DO YOU KNOW . . .

- How to tell when they're trying?
- How to spot a stiff?
- How to read the trainer's mind?
- How to tell when they're *not* betting?
- How to pick the "mudders"?
- How to tell which races to pass?
- How to throw out sure-fire losers?
- How to bet different kinds of races?
- How to beat *any race that's fit to play?*

These and a hundred other tricky questions are answered in

SMART HANDICAPPING MADE EASY

by WILLIAM BAUMAN

Here is a book that goes farther than anything you have ever read on the secrets of the professionals. Most books on handicapping fall down when they tackle the all-important question of whether or not a horse is going to *try*—whether the stable is sending the horse today or prepping him for a race next week. *Smart Handicapping Made Easy* tells you how to answer that crucial question, and tells you when to bet a horse and when to lay off.

If there were no wagering on races, and trainers therefore had no motive for *manipulating* animals to get a price, the horse-players would find it a lot easier to dope the winners. A good handicapper could read the past performances and come up with the contenders almost every time. But as things stand, "pure" handicapping is never good enough to put a player on the winning side of the fence.

Smart Handicapping Made Easy ties up "pure" handicapping with the inside betting activity of professionals, so that a player can know when to get aboard and when to lay off.

Here is a book on the art of playing the races intelligently that will save you money from the start and put you on the road to success. It is a complete manual for the smart operator, yet it is written so simply that any beginner can learn all he needs to know about the game. And both beginners and dyed-in-the wool players will find eye-openers on every page.

SMART
HANDICAPPING
MADE
EASY

by WILLIAM BAUMAN

Published by
Melvin Powers
WILSHIRE BOOK COMPANY
12015 Sherman Road
No. Hollywood, California 91605
Telephone: (213) 875-1711 / (818) 983-1105

Published by arrangement with Citadel Press
(a subsidiary of Lyle Stuart, Inc.)

Seventh paperbound printing, 1972
Copyright © 1960 by William Bauman
All rights reserved
Citadel Press, Inc., Publishers
A subsidiary of Lyle Stuart, Inc.
120 Enterprise Avenue
Secaucus, New Jersey 07094
Manufactured in the United States of America

ISBN 0-87980-270-7

CONTENTS

For ROSEMARY ELLEN

"After all, horse sense is just stable thinking."
OLD PROVERB

SMART HANDICAPPING MADE EASY

1. THE CRYSTAL BALL

SUPPOSE THAT ONE fine day you go to the track and start
weaving your way among the assorted touts, each with a
fistful of tip sheets, who line up about the entrance gates and
try to sell you a bill of goods for a buck.

You shrug them off, knowing they can't pick winners any
better than you can, and probably not as well, or they would
be inside the track getting well on their own selections, instead of standing in the hot sun peddling their miserable
cards for a few dollars a day.

But, strangely, from among these touts a little man with
no cards to sell walks up and says, "Mac, I've got something
in my pocket I'd like to show you. Don't jump when I tell
you what it is. . . . It's a little crystal ball. If you look into it
carefully before each race you will see something that might
do you a lot of good."

Naturally, you think he's crazy, but for the laughs you go
with him, away from the crowd. And to your amazement he
pulls out of his pocket something about the size of an
orange—indeed a crystal ball, in which as on a small television screen, you can already see horses charging down the
stretch, their colors flashing in the sunlight!

As a horse-player, you are accustomed to surprises, to
strange happenings, and to the topsy-turvy world of the race
track, but you have to admit this is the *most!*

Before you can get your breath, the little man, grinning all over, says, "Yes, Mac, that's the first race today: It will be running in about a half-hour."

Bowled over as you are, you nevertheless shout out the obvious question: *"Does it show you the winner?"*

The grin fades from the little man's weather-beaten face. He suddenly looks at you with disgust and puts the ball back into his pocket. "Mac," he says, "I don't know whether I can do business with you. You're one of those guys who believes in miracles. Maybe you better go over there and buy one of them tip sheets."

At this point you are all shook up, and maybe even getting a little sore. So you say sharply, "If the darn thing doesn't show you the winner, what good is it?"

"Easy, Mac," the man says, pulling out the ball again and shading it with his hand. "Look carefully this time. Take a *good* look."

You peer intently into the ball, and what you seem to see is a repeated re-run of the stretch finish of a race. There are about eight horses running through the ball and you can see the numbers on the saddle pads of those who are not up front, because they are all strung out behind the closely-packed contenders, who are crossing the wire together, so that a photo-finish is certainly indicated.

"It shows you pretty clearly who the losers are, Old Man," you exclaim, "but it doesn't separate the horses on top."

"Of course not, Mac," he says, "Not even a crystal ball can tell you *the* winner of a horse race! Don't you know that yet?"

Getting more irritated, you say sourly, "I still don't see where that ball is much help."

"All right—there are eight horses in this first race," the Old Man says, with a trace of anger, "and the ball shows you that No. 1, No. 8, No. 5, No. 3 and No. 2 are *not* winning the race. Then who is winning it? Even *you* ought to be able to figure that out—the horses crossing the wire together are No. 4, No. 6 and No. 7."

"I see," you say, beginning to see.

"Now read me the odds on those three horses," the Old Man says.

You look at the morning line on the program and say, "No. 4 is three to one; No. 6 is five to one and No. 7 is ten to one."

The Old Man grins again: "You catch on quick, Mac. Now do you buy the ball or don't you?"

2. A BATTLE OF WITS

"You can't beat the races, it's a sucker's game and horse-players all die broke!" Does that sound familiar? Of course it does. You hear it everywhere. *Everybody* says it.

Most people seem to have fixed ideas, or moral prejudices, about playing the horses and about horse-players. The horse-player, when he is not considered a menace, is looked upon as a comic figure who ought to be the fall guy in a Grade B movie. Who hasn't heard the one about the chronic horse-player who, returning from the track, jubilantly tells his friend: "Man, I was *lucky* today! I broke even—and I really needed the money!"

But apart from all this, there may be another reason for Everybody's attitude toward horse-playing. Everybody is the public—Joe Blow, who from time to time has gone to a race track and tried to root home a winner.

Most people are speaking from experience. They have seen it happen time and again that when they bet the even-money favorite—a twenty-to-one shot comes romping home on top, while their highly recommended animal finishes second, third or even worse. And then, getting fed-up, they have bet a twenty-to-one shot in the next race, only to see the even-money favorite win by three lengths.

To make matters worse, when Joe bets them to win, they

place; when he bets them to place, they show, and when he bets them to show, they finish "up the track."

Nothing could be more disgusting—or expensive.

Yes, Joe speaks from experience, and he knows what he is talking about. He is talking about *himself*. He is saying, "*I* can't beat the races."

But Joe doesn't put it that way. When he talks about the horses he is not content to talk only about himself. Since misery loves company, he tries to generalize, give moral advice, and say that *you* can't beat them either, that *nobody* can beat them. He says in lofty tones, "You can't beat the horses!"

But this is where he is dead wrong—just as wrong as when he made his last wager on a horse race and lost. For, he overlooks the simple arithmetic of the parimutuel machines, the obvious law of displacement—that what goes in must come out, less the 15% track take. Joe forgets that there could be no losers like himself, if there were not at the same time some winners, not like himself.

If he had said, "Most people can't beat the races," he would have been saying something almost as true as the law of gravitation. For, let's face it, the collective public can't do it, never could and never will. In fact, it is *impossible*, precisely because of the 15% take, plus the breakage, which the track and the state tax scoop out of every betting pool. The Sport of Kings is big business, and the public pays for its recreation. *But what is impossible to the collective public is perfectly possible to you, the individual.* Providing you can put yourself into that minority faction which cashes the winning tickets.

You are the person who reads this book. You have at least average intelligence, you have some money to bet and you either have or must develop a measure of self-control.

For parimutuel betting is a battle of wits and self-discipline between you and the mass of horse-players gathered at a race track. When you win you not only outguess or outsmart them, you perform an act of self-control in keeping a level head, in making just the right bets in the right spots and at the right times. When *you* win, *they* lose!

In fact, when you start winning you will discover something that may seem very strange to you. You won because you did just about the opposite of what the public does. You won because you did the opposite of what you yourself might do "naturally." But this is not strange at all, it only seems so. For how else could you be a winner in a parimutuel betting system, in which the collective public is bound to lose!

Everybody can beat a single race once in a while. Joe Blow might even make a lucky stab and hit the Daily Double —but he'll lose it all back tomorrow, or next week, with the iron certainty of a law of nature.

The trick is not to beat a single race—but to beat almost any race that's fit to play!

3. THE THIRD MAN

HORSE-PLAYING IS a battle of wits between you and the mass of horse-players.

However, in this war, as in those ancient battles between Jewish tribes, there is a Very Important Person who stands behind the scenes and pulls a few strings. This mysterious fellow is never seen by the public, and, because he is never seen he is very often underestimated or even forgotten entirely. And when a horse-player ignores this dignitary, he is inviting trouble just as surely as the Israelites invited a thunderbolt from Jehovah!

This third party is the Trainer. In some cases he may also be the owner. But whatever he is, he is the man who runs the horse in a given race *with the intention of trying to win, or with some other intention.*

To put it more clearly we can say that the Third Man *at times sends his horse out to win, and that at other times he runs his horse not to win, but to achieve some other purpose.*

When a horse is not scratched—when he runs in a race—we must ask this question: "What is the horse doing in the race?"

The failure to ask himself this question is the No. 1 reason that keeps Joe Blow from cashing winning tickets at a race track. Joe forgets about, or doesn't even think about the Third Man.

It is truly pathetic, but Joe Blow dumps thousands of dollars down the drain every day betting horses that are not even trying to win—horses that the trainer is not "sending." These horses are "out for the air" (the exercise), or they are "running for Sweeney."

Now it is true that the trainer does not have absolute control over the performance of his animal, or his jockey, once the race is off—and that his face gets very red, on rare occasions, when the beast does just the opposite of what was expected. It wins when it was not "sent," or when it was supposed not to have a chance. This happens once in a while around a race track, but it mainly happens in old silent movies or in television soap operas.

When the trainer makes a mistake it is usually in the other direction—he thinks he *can* win in a spot where he *can't*. Who doesn't overrate his own dog or his own baby?

We don't mean to say that all this is dishonest or "crooked," because it isn't. A lot of it is merely "trade practice." Training and racing horses is a business, and every business has its trade secrets, and special angles for survival in the heat of competition.

It costs a lot of money to feed a race horse, pay the barn bill, the trainer, the jockey, the veterinarian, the exercise boy, the entrance fee, etc. And, except in the better type of races, purse money paid to winners is very inadequate. How many horses pay their own keep with purse winnings? The answer might astound the general public. . . . So, if it doesn't come from this source, where does it come from? It comes from the stable itself betting the horse when he wins. And when he wins, which is never very often, it is naturally desirable that he win at the highest possible odds.

Why is the trainer not trying to win every time he sends his horse to the post? The more you try, the more races you win, you might say. . . . Well it doesn't quite work out that way in the case of the cheaper claiming animals, who make up the bulk of the barn population at any race track, and who are the hard core of the racing business. There are hundreds of these animals filling up track programs compared with the mere dozens of *good* horses who go in the allowance, handicap and stakes features, where the purse cream is heavy to very rich.

It might actually be more profitable for a trainer with a cheap horse to win one race at a mutuel price of 10 to 1, than to win several races at very short odds. A horse is not ready to win every time he goes to the post, so that on those few occasions when he *is*, the trainer must make the most of it.

Remember that predicting *the* winner of a horse race is always a very difficult thing, even for the Third Man, and that when he "sends" his horse he wants to feel that the spot is just right and that his chances are *extremely* good. Otherwise, if he "sends" the animal, and it just misses, or runs third or fourth, the odds will be spoiled for the next attempt or even the next several attempts. Today he was 10 to 1—next Tuesday, when he runs again, as a result of his top-notch effort today he might be 2 to 1. The trainer has "tipped his mitt," as they say, and the public handicappers are quick to point out that the animal is "improving" or that he is "ready to win." This spoils the lemonade.

Suppose that you owned a horse that you knew was "hot," that is, ready to win a race, provided you can get him into a soft spot. You enter him in a claiming event for cheapsters and eagerly await the official list of entries. When you finally get this sheet your face falls five inches. For, guess what? Entered in the same race are at least two beetles who have beaten you time and again. Either you didn't know they were eligible, or they were just carted in from another oval. Your horse "Tootsie Roll" simply cannot beat "Bertha's Baby," much less the gelding "Lonesome Oscar," or "Nasty Nancy," a miserable mare who is *hot* right now, and beating everything in sight.

You can scratch your horse out of the race, which might be the wise thing to do. However, this is risky too, for the beast might just cool off on you before you can get him into the right spot. By running him, you try to keep him at peak. *Because he wants to run!* Well, you decide to let him go out on the track.

So, then, what do you do? Tell your jockey to ride hell-for-leather and try to beat them? And almost surely wind up third or fourth or even worse—and at the same time tip off the public that your animal is in sharp shape, so that next time, *when you really can win in a featherbed spot,* you will get a price of even money.

Well, there may be a trainer or two around who would do this, but their ranks are thin, since they go broke fast. Most trainers tell the jockey what to do. They don't say, "Pull the horse," or anything like that. When they want to blow a race, they say, "Lay off the pace," or "Don't use the bat," or anything else that doesn't make sense.

It is only when a horse is a "hot" public choice that a trainer may hesitate to run him "stiff" and thus lay himself wide open for the wrath of the Track Stewards. These stewards know that honesty is also good business, and they like to see the public choice win, or give a decent account of himself. Whereas, if a horse is 2-1, or 3-1, and turns in a dismal effort, that's another matter. Maybe the animal *figured* to lose!

Most horses have to be brought into form and kept in

condition by actual racing. It is only by running them in races that you can keep them fit, just as an athlete must be kept moving while in training. Small stables do not have private race tracks on which to train their horses against other horses. Morning workouts are never a substitute for an actual race. So, very frequently a horse is in a race for no other reason than the excerise. *He is not ready to win, and since he is not ready, he is not being sent.*

The trainer won't "send" a horse if he thinks the spot is too tough, or if the animal is sore or out of form. So far, so simple.

But very often the trainer has a few jokers up his sleeve. For instance, he will run his horse in a *tough spot* because he wants to make the animal look bad for the next race—when he will drop it down in class and shoot for the target at a fancy mutuel price. The public sees how badly the horse was beaten the last time out and won't touch him this time. This is exactly what the Third Man counts on. He might get 10, 15 or even 20 to 1, if he can turn the trick.

Sometimes the trainer will run his horse in bad footing when he knows the animal can't possibly win in the mud— for the same reason; namely, to make him look bad to the public when he "sends" the horse on a fast track.

The same things applies in the matter of distance. A trainer who has a sprinter on his hands that won't go more than five or six furlongs will often enter this animal at one mile or more, just to make him look bad, to build up his odds for the day when the beast will go out and run the race of his life at six furlongs.

And vice versa, a router may run back a number of times at six furlongs and then, when the price is right, he will go at a mile or more and win like a champion.

It is not always this tricky, or even tricky at all. It is

sometimes a matter of conditioning. A sprinter may be showing signs of quitting even in a short race. By running him a route a few times, the theory is that you build up his endurance for a sprint race. And by running a router a few times in a sprint race, you may get the horse into the habit of running in the early part of the race, where he has been lagging and getting himself outrun.

If the Third Man finds his horse, a slow-breaking animal, in No. 1 post position, he may not try to win the race, since his horse is at a disadvantage. This animal, who comes from behind, will usually have to circle the field in order to win. That is, he will have to run farther than some of the others. The trainer may not want to risk wasting a "hot" animal.

On a half-mile, or five-eighths-mile track, the trainer may not try if his horse draws an *outside* post position where he will be forced to run wide because of the sharp turns and the short stretches. While it can be done, it is usually pretty difficult to win from Post Position 10 on one of these "bull ring" tracks.

Now, we do not wish to give the impression that a trainer is *always* manipulating his horse, because very often he is not. When it seems that an animal *can* win in a given spot, and the mutuel price is fair enough, there is no reason to assume the trainer is not sending the animal. If a horse has been going off in his last few starts at a good price, running with his own kind, at a suitable distance, over a track that is not to his distaste, we can assume that the trainer has been trying. And if the same holds true for today's race, we can assume he is trying today.

Also, when a horse is in good form, and winning, a trainer will naturally try to win as many races as he can while the good form lasts. Even when the price on the odds board is extremely low. For, after all, purse money is never passed up without a good reason.

It is when an animal has been losing because of being raced over his head, or at a wrong distance, or on an unsuitable track, etc., that we must be on guard and suspect monkey-business. This is especially true when the mutual price today is only, say 6-1, as against 15-1 or higher in a previous effort. Here, we must pull ourselves up sharp and pay attention. For today, with the horse slipped into a spot where he belongs, the stable may be betting.

And, likewise, when an animal lost last time in a spot that seemed right for him, and the mutuel price was even-money, 2-1 or 3-1, as against 6-1, 8-1, or more today the animal may be sent for the marbles, this time.

So, this brings us to a very important angle for picking losers! It is clear that if a trainer is not going to try with his horse, and if we can determine this by putting two and two together—then we can eliminate this animal from the picture. Nothing could be more important from the standpoint of finding the contenders in a horse race!

I agree, you say, but how does it help me? How can I tell when the trainer is trying and when he isn't?

That's a very good question, and one we are going to answer in the next chapter, which deals with another angle for looking into the crystal ball.

The role of the Third Man must be understood, because unless you are alert to this gent's intentions not all the angles in the world will do you any good. For this is the Major Angle, and the horse-player who ignores it is in no fit state of mind to be playing the races. He hasn't got a Chinaman's chance of winning, and his trips to the track will be remembered, not as pleasant times, but as "Death in the Afternoon."

As we proceed, we will deal again and again with these tricks or strategems (often merely plain horse sense) that trainers live by, and sometimes make killings with—matters which the public pays very little attention to. And because Joe Blow pays so little attention, this is your opportunity!

4. THE VOICE OF THE TOTE BOARD

AT MOST RACE tracks there is a public address system over which a voice describes the running of each race. This voice sends a player's blood pressure up when the horse he has bet takes the lead at the head of the stretch, and then puts him into a cold sweat as some other animal gets a call as fourth and moving up, as they all charge down to the finish wire. This voice is so loud that very few players ever fail to hear it—not even with all the shouting of the crowd.

This voice tells you what is happening *while* it is happening.

However, at every race track, there is a second voice— a small, sly voice—that tries to tell you what is *going* to happen, *before* it happens!

This is the Voice of the Tote Board, which, like the Delphic Oracle, speaks in riddles, never saying anything directly or plainly, but predicting the future nevertheless.

If you have to be crazy to hear a silent voice, then it is safe to say that the collective public at a race track is a very sane group of people on the whole, because it hears nothing at all of this second voice. Only a small minority hears it, a minority which is crazy like a fox!

What does the Tote Board tell us when we learn to listen? Certainly not *the* winner. While the Tote Board is the champion handicapper of them all, it comes up with *the* winner only about 33% of the time. This is the rough per-centage of times the post-time favorite (the lowest-priced horse on the Board) wins the race.

Since it is impossible to beat the races consistently by flat-betting the post-time favorite—what good then is this Voice of the Tote Board? What does it say that will help us?

It says a mouthful! But, like the Greek oracle, it says nothing *specific*. It speaks the general truth! And if we know how to *use* the general truth, we know more than most of the horse-players at a race track.

By the general truth we do not mean that low-priced horses are likely to be winners and long-priced horses likely to be losers. Not at all. If it were this simple, all horse-players would die rich.

The important thing the Tote Board can tell us is whether or not the Third Man is trying today—whether a given animal is being sent for the sugar or is simply out for the ozone!

In the preceding chapter we pointed out that stables with cheap horses (that is, the overwhelming majority of stables) would have a rough time trying to meet expenses, much less build up a bank account, if they had to depend on purse-money winnings only. And that consequently they had to bet their winning animals to stay in the game and prosper. This is an economic fact, and we care little about such statements to the contrary that are issued to the newspapers about this stable or that stable not being a "betting stable." There *is* such a thing as a non-betting stable, no doubt, but it would have to be a very rich man's stable (which would not be likely to have cheap horses in it) or the stable of an eccentric owner or trainer.

We cannot be concerned with such exceptions to the rule because they exert no significant influence on our strategy.

For our purposes, you can take it for granted that all stables or stable connections are interested in maneuvering a horse into a spot where he can win at good odds—and betting this beetle on that fine day when it is *sent*!

Therefore, if we can hear the Tote Board correctly and detect this inside betting activity, we will know when a particular horse is going out on the track to bust a gut trying to win. But, likewise—and this is more important—when we cannot detect this inside betting activity, *because there is none,* then we can rest assured that a particular horse is going out on the track to limber up his legs and inhale the fresh air. Nothing more.

We might summarize it this way:

(A) Horses on which there is inside betting action will be sent.

(B) Horses on which there is no inside betting action will not be sent—usually.

Why do we say "usually," in this latter instance?

Because there is such a thing as a stable betting its money with bookmakers instead of through the parimutuel machines at the track. If the money is bet with bookmakers, perhaps in another city, then such money will not get into the machines and depress the mutual pay-off. At least, that's what the stable hopes. Strangely enough, however, this money has a way of getting back to the track. Bookmakers are not exactly stupid people, and when they see a lot of money showing on an animal, they hustle it to the track one way or another, even if the track is half-way across the country. By getting the money, or part of it, back to the point of origin, they soften the blow on their own heads, by driving down the odds.

How do we go about detecting inside betting or the lack of it on a particular horse in a given race?

Public handicappers, while they have a hard time picking

winners, are usually pretty shrewd fellows when it comes to setting up a line of approximate odds on a given race. This is also true of the track handicapper, who sets up a "morning line" at the race track.

Of all the people who guess at the odds a horse will have in a given race, the track handicapper is far and away the most reliable. For, he has the advantage of knowing which horse are scratched out of a race. He does not make his line until he knows which horses are going to run. This, plus his general knowledge of the horses and trainers around *his* race track, gives him a very good "feel" about what a particular horse should be in line. He is in a far better position to do this than a public handicapper for a racing paper, who must make up his line the day before without knowing just which horses will run.

So, if the track handicapper feels that a horse should be 20-1 today, and we find that when the betting gets under way the animal is only 5-1—then it may be that the stable is betting. *Especially if this horse is not picked to win or run close by the public handicappers in the* Daily Racing Form *or the* Morning Telegraph. . . . Conversely, if the track handicapper feels that a horse should be 3-1 or less today, and we find that he has in fact gone to 15 or 20-1—then it may be that the stable is *not betting,* and therefore *not sending* the animal, probably because he hasn't got a chance of winning.

These examples are extreme cases, of course, but we want to make the point that deviations either way from the track handicapper's feeling about the odds on a horse ought to be a signal for further investigation of this particular beast. The mere fact that the odds go up or down *is not conclusive.* We must dig deeper.

Part of the folklore of racing is that the public makes an animal the favorite in a given race, or that the public makes the prices on all the horses. If we mean that public money does this, then it is a correct statement. But public insight or public shrewdness does not do it!

The track handicapper and public handicappers, especially those in the *Daily Racing Form,* play the biggest role in steering the public on or off certain horses and in setting the odds picture.

This flow of public money *on the opinion of the public handicappers,* is the most powerful flow of money into the parimutuel machines, so that when that other but less powerful current, the stable and professional betting, succeeds in driving down the price on an "unselected" horse, say by 100%, you can rest assured the bet was substantial and that the animal will be in there fighting.

Sometimes a "hot tip" will circulate among the public at a track and cause a great wave of emotional betting on a certain beast, thus driving up the odds on the other animals. This emotional betting is very often dead wrong, and based on false information, deliberately put out by professionals who are betting something else in the race and getting an abnormally high mutuel pay-off because of this public stupidity.

We must distinguish this kind of madness of the crowd from the more deliberate betting by the professionals. If you watch the Tote Board carefully and mark each series of flashing changes in the line on your program, you can usually detect professional betting. This money is dumped into the machines very early, and shows as a sharp *first* drop, from the morning line; or it is dumped in very late, as the horses are going to the post, and shows as a sharp *last-minute* drop—or it is slowly fed into the machine, *a little at a time,* so as not to "tip the mitt." It has no emotional character about it. It is very deliberate, as opposed to the public hysteria which sends a horse's price down with every change on the board.

Just before post-time (which is the only sensible time *ever* to make a bet at a race track) analyze what has happened on the Tote Board and you will get a final picture and see how public betting has been modified by the professional betting to produce the closing odds.

The figures might follow a pattern something like this:

Horse No.	Type of Animal	Morning Line	First Change	Second Change	Latest Change
No. 1	(Hot Horse)	2	3	4	8/5
No. 2	(Public Choice)	3	2	8/5	2
No. 3	(Dead Horse)	12	15	20	30
No. 4	(Live Horse)	15	6	8	12
No. 5	(Wake-up Horse)	10	6	6	6
No. 6	(The Stiff)	4	5	6	9
No. 7	(The Decoy)	20	10	5	5/2

The above figures are not intended to be a scientific representation of a true spread or change of odds but are set down to illustrate the Tote Board characteristics of certain typical animals. Here is the way we would analyze this picture:

No. 1 (Hot Horse)   This horse, which was probably picked second by the track or public handicappers, is definitely being sent today, although this did not become apparent until the last change on the Board. The money was dumped in the machines late to prevent the public's getting on the bandwagon.

No. 2 (Public Choice)

This animal was obviously the track or public handicappers' choice and therefore the public bet him very heavily all along the line. If last-minute money had not been dumped on No. 1 this horse would have been the post-time favorite. This type of horse is usually out to win because he *can* win.

No. 3 (Dead Horse)

This animal was picked by no handicapper and there is no evidence of inside betting. He is in the race, but he is not in there to win, but for some other reason.

No. 4 (Live Horse)

This animal was picked by no handicapper but there *is* evidence of stable betting. The money was dumped in early, so as not to be detected, and the price has drifted back up to about what it should be. This animal will be trying all the way, although he may not be good enough to get there.

No. 5 (Wake-Up Horse)

This animal was not picked by any handicapper, and the public at large did not bet him. The stable, however, has bet him, gradually, so as to give no tip-off. This is proved by the fact that his odds dropped and then held low throughout all changes at only 6/1. He will try hard.

No. 6 (The Stiff)   This animal was picked third or fourth by the handicappers, perhaps even to win by one of them. The stable, however, knows he can't win and hasn't bet a dime. In fact, they hope somebody will claim the horse.

No. 7 (The Decoy)   This animal was not picked by the handicappers and for good reasons. He is an unsound beast, and yet he has been "tipped" loudly to the public. Why? When a stable is out to win they keep it a secret. So, the only conclusion is that some other horse in the race is the one being sent.

This is part of the general truth the Tote Board can tell us. These examples are by no means complete and the interpretations we have given are not meant to be final or conclusive. As far as this type of analysis goes, it is good, but it is not good enough!

We must go further and make absolutely sure that the betting we think we have detected on a horse, or horses, is truly *inside* betting and not the result of some public fancy or the whim of a desperate nut loaded with dough.

But even more important—we must make absolutely sure that what we think is a lack of betting action on a given horse is truly a lack of betting action. For it is possible that a stable bet can be snowed under—obscured—by heavy public betting on other horses.

The mere fact that the odds on a horse drift upwards does not for certain mean that the stable has not bet the animal.

A horse can go up in price today and still be lower than he should be in relation to his recent performance. Also, a horse can become a true *overlay* when emotional betting on other horses is in progress.

Contrary to what the public thinks, most of the stunning longshots that come down at box-car figures are horses which were both *sent* and *bet!*

The Voice of the Tote Board speaks a wise language to those who can hear, and it should be emphasized that the Third Man has a vested interest in making his horse look bad to the public. Many so-called "In-and-Outers" are "in" when the price is right and "out" when it isn't. So, we must never pick a horse as a loser just because he happens to be a longshot; or as a contender just because he is a short price or a public choice, or just because the odds rise or fall.

So, in order to put the double-check clincher on what we think we detect about inside betting, we must go to the past performance charts* and see what the Tote Board said about a horse last time out, or last few times out. By comparing the price on an animal today with the price he went off at previously, *and under what conditions,* we can go beyond the general truth and arrive at the specific truth.

In other words, we can *know* that a certain animal will be

* We are assuming that you have had *some* experience, however limited, in looking over the past performances of the horses listed for each race in such publications as the *Daily Racing Form* or the *Morning Telegraph*. If you do not know how to read these Past Performances or the Official Charts which provide a description of the race, send your name and address, along with five-cents in stamps to cover handling and mailing to the *Daily Racing Form*, 731 Plymouth Ct., Chicago 5, Illinois, and they will send you free of charge by return mail a 20-page booklet which explains the meaning of every symbol, abbreviation and figure used in the tables and charts.

in there today trying for all he is worth—*and therefore may be an actual contender*—but that another horse *will certainly be a loser* because he is not even going to try! In short, many races list some horses we can pick as losers—automatically!

If the Third Man angle is the Major Angle, then the Tote Board Angle is the Minor Angle. The two must be viewed together—always—and always together with the five past performance factors explained in the following pages.

For it is only by connecting up the Voice of the Tote Board with what we see in the past performances as to a horse's relative chance in a given race—that we know we are reading the trainer's thoughts and intentions correctly.

This strategy narrows a field of horses down to the *possible* contenders by eliminating the sure-fire losers and at the same time throws a strong light on the question of which among the honest ones are likely to be the *actual* contenders.

Here, in essence, is the secret of all smart handicapping!

5. DOWN ON THE FORM

JUST BEFORE THE RUNNING of a big stakes race, a woman stepped up to a famous trainer and said, "Mr. Jones, I *know* your horse is going to win because he is the prettiest one in the race."

The worried trainer looked at her sourly and replied, "Madam, this is no beauty contest."

No, winning horse races has very little in common with winning beauty contests—except perhaps in one respect. When a beauty wins a local contest, she is then pushed on to sterner competition in bigger cities. Similarly, a race horse, when he wins a few contests, is pushed on to tougher and tougher spots. This is inherent in our track handicapping and race-eligibilty system.

As a horse wins races he must carry more and more weight and run in better races. He can start out in a $2,000 claiming event, carrying 110 pounds and show such progressive ability that he might find himself in a $5,000 claiming race, carrying perhaps 120 pounds. He may then meet his Waterloo and have to start back down the ladder.

This system is used by all race tracks and it is designed to keep one horse, or one stable, from winning all the chips. On the whole, it is very effective in achieving this end.

Just as winning horses are pushed into tougher spots, so

do losing horses slide into softer spots—by the same track handicapping system. Just a little reflection will show you how this tends to spread the purse money around. It is a good thing and it makes most races pretty open contests.

At this point all comparisons with a beauty contest end. Because while a beauty may move up and down, from soft to hard spots, and vice versa, just like a horse, she does not usually, from week to week, get more beautiful or less beautiful. If she did, you can imagine how hard it would be to guess the winner beforehand.

Well, horses don't get more or less beautiful as they move up and down in class, but they do get more or less swift, more or less strong, more or less stubborn. They are usually on the upgrade or on the downgrade of what has been called the Form Cycle. So in the case of horses you have two series of moving conditions—the condition of the race as set down by the track handicapper and the condition of the animal itself; that is, his physical condition. This is what makes picking *the* winner of a horse race so difficult.

Just because the above sounds complicated, you should not allow yourself to think it's as complicated as it sounds. Because it isn't, despite the many books, complete with graphs, charts, and curves, that have been published on the subject.

While there is such a thing as a "form cycle" it cannot be studied in the abstract, apart from an animal's past performances in a certain class, his basic speed, his preferred distance, his footing likes and dislikes and the spots he had been running in. In other words the Form Cycle reveals itself only in the actual past performance of a horse, and, it is important to add, *only when the horse is trying.*

Furthermore, and this is extremely important, it is the average horse-player's confused notions about a horse being "in form" or "out of form" that keeps him from cashing winning tickets. Next to Joe Blow's ignorance of the shenanigans of the Third Man, it is his faulty ideas of "form" that are responsible for his many defeats at the track. If he is not a form reader, then "tips" will do the same thing for him.

"I've got a hot tip," Joe tells his friend. "The trainer told me that his colt 'Morning Glory' is really in sharp shape." Once in a long while you cash a winning ticket as a result of hearing, or overhearing, such "inside information"—but you know better than anybody else that you have torn up the tickets ten times for every time you didn't.

Actually, the "information" might have been straight. The colt might have been truly in condition, and ready to win, but the conditions of the race itself sent him down to defeat. For it is not enough that a horse be in sharp shape to win a race. He must be in shape and the spot must be soft enough for him to get there! In some races all the contenders are in "sharp shape," and there is probably a "tip" out on each and every one of them.

The only thing a trainer can tell you that's worth listening to—is whether or not he's trying. The same thing goes for a jockey (who may not even know this much!). And even when they're trying, never forget, they are still a long way from home. In short, they still have to get there—and this is seldom easy.

Remember that even a well-meant horse will lose if the Third Man himself uses bad judgment and "sends" him in a race where he will be *overmatched* or *outrun,* or *when the distance or track condition is unsuitable*—that is to say, when the trainer places the animal in a tough spot.

Horses *do* come into form and go out of form, but they are not so inconsistent as the public thinks. If they were not manipulated so much, they would seem to run in a more reasonable manner. Horses are more consistent than most people—and far more consistent than most trainers. The public has been fooled in this matter so long that it now takes its own confusion for granted and mistakes the condition of a horse with the condition of the race.

A beauty may look like a queen in Podunk, but may look rather sorry in Atlantic City. So much is clear. But it is also true that a queen in Podunk may look bad even in Bodunk, another whistle stop. A $2,000 claiming horse may run a sorry race at $10,000. Everybody knows that. But he may also run a sorry race from one $2,000 heat to another $2,000 heat. Why? Because every race is different, not only as to the track handicapper's conditions, but to the natural conditions of mixing up the competition, which causes each race to be run differently. And the *way* a race is run has a great bearing on its outcome.

What are some of the mistaken notions about Form—notions time-honored by the general public and some public handicappers? You will find that almost all of them center about the number of lengths a horse has been losing by in his most recent previous races, or the number of lengths he has been winning by. That is, a horse is thought to be "cold" when running back, or "hot" when running close up—and especially "hot" when winning.

Of course, in some cases this is absolutely correct—but, and this is a big but—more often than not, it is dead wrong! To judge a horse's chances today by the number of lengths he lost by, or won by, last start, or even last several starts—is the greatest weakness of all superficial form players among the public, and the greatest failing of most public handicappers, who do not have the time to study carefully each and every race, and thus do not get beyond the obvious and deceptive surface appearances in any given race.

Every race is different. There are no two races alike. What a horse does in one race is no guarantee of what he will do in another. It is only when the conditions are approximately identical, and this doesn't happen too often, that you can rely on the obvious.

Do not, as the general public does, confuse the condition of the race with the condition of the horse. Before we decide whether a horse is off-form today, we must look at the animal's recent previous races and ask the following questions. Never allow losing margins (even 20 lengths) or winning margins to influence your judgment until you consider these other factors.

Was the animal losing or running back *because he was off-form*, or because:

> *He was overmatched?*
> *He was outrun because of a hot pace?*
> *He was going the wrong distance?*
> *He was not favored by the track or track condition?*

Before we can determine that a horse is "off form" in the true sense of the word, or that he has not yet reached his best form to be a contender in a particular race, or that he is on the "downgrade," that is, falling off from his good form and now on a down-cycle—*we must see him in the framework of these other factors.*

When we eliminate an animal from a given race, we must know why we are doing so—because if we eliminate him for the wrong reason we will almost certainly get ourselves into trouble.

What looked like "bad form," for instance, might have been a false appearance. The animal could have been in the best of shape but was entered with horses too classy for him. Today, with his own kind, he might show brilliant "form." Or, the trouble might have been an especially hot pace that left him flat-footed, and the jockey didn't thereafter persevere. Or, maybe the distance or the "track" was wrong. Today is a new day, a new race, and a new set of conditions. *Today*, it might be a different story!

So, we must never make up our mind too quickly and decide that any one thing is wrong until we look at all five of the past performance factors, and cross-check one against the other.

(See chapter 13, chart studies A and B.)

Use these "off-form" angles (*but only in connection with other factors*) for spotting well-meant horses and for picking sure-fire losers:

A. If an animal which has been running "dead"—showing no particular pep or speed at any stage of his recent races —and these races have seemed "right" for him, with a fair mutuel price on the Board, we can pick him as a loser today if the mutuel price today does not appear significantly lower than the mutuel price he went off at in those previous races, or if we detect no Tote Board action. *LOSER.*

B. If an animal which has been winning, or racing close up, suddenly begins in his most recent races to reveal a tendency to lag at the start, or to "stop," where previously he got off well, or went on with courage—we can pick him as a loser today, if the mutuel price today is significantly higher than it was in his recent races, or if there seems to be an absence of inside betting. *LOSER.*

C. If an animal has been showing some "life" at some stage of his recent races—that is, early speed, or late speed, or running evenly where he ran "dead" or in spots only—we cannot automatically pick him as a loser today. In fact, in the case of such an animal, we must proceed very carefully, for he may be coming right into a winning effort. This is especially true if the mutuel price today is lower than in those previous efforts—or regardless of the mutuel price if we can detect inside betting. *POSSIBILITY*.

D. If an animal which has been running "dead" or sluggishly in his recent races nevertheless shows a series of sparkling work-outs, then he may be coming into form on the training track and may suddenly "burst" into form with a wining effort, especially if the mutuel price today is lower than in the recent races, or if we can detect inside betting. *POSSIBILITY*.

E. If an animal which has been running just so-so in his recent races, but has been claimed recently, and has not won or shown any sharp form since that time, we cannot automatically pick him as a loser—because whenever one man claim's another man's horse, it is usually because he knows the animal is "on the upgrade." And this is especially true when we can *now* detect Tote action on the animal. *POSSIBILITY*.

(*See chapter 14, examples 1, 2, 4, and 8.*)

As a horse wins a certain number of races, or a certain amount of money (this naturally varies from track to track) he is pushed into tougher and tougher spots, by getting more weight to carry, or into tougher and tougher company, by finding himself eligible only for better claiming events or higher-type allowance or handicap events.

Claiming races are races in which you enter your horse at a specified price (it may range from $1,000 at a cheap track to $20,000 or more at a better track). They are supposedly kept honest by the fact that somebody can claim your horse and take him away at the stated price. This is to discourage running a good $10,000 horse, say, for only $2,000, and thus copping the purse. However, nowadays there are "optional" claiming races, in which the horse cannot be claimed.

Allowance races are races in which the horse is not "on the block," that is, cannot be claimed. They are usually better-type races than claiming events, with richer purse money. Of course, allowance races at one track, (a cheap track), may have horses in it worth only about $2,000, while at a top track they may be worth $30,000 or more. In these races losing animals are allowed weight off.

Handicap races are races in which the track handicapper assigns weight to the competing animals according to his estimate of their ability. They are usually for pretty good horses (this too, varies with the track). *Stakes races,* in which the owners of the horses have previously put up a certain amount of cash to become eligible, are the best type races of all.

6. FLUNKING THE CLASS

RACING IS CALLED the Sport of Kings because royal families of old seem to have been fascinated with class and courage in a horse—in the beginning perhaps for military reasons but later on for the sheer sport of pitting one thoroughbred against another and usually wagering on the outcome.

Queen Anne of England is given much of the credit for standardizing the breeding of horses. About 1750, she ruled that a certain number of stallions and brood mares be selected as the founders of a family of "thoroughbred horses," that is, horses whose blood lines could be traced back directly to Arabia. Later on, in 1791, when the English Jockey Club created the Stud Book, this idea was carried out.

The "thoroughbred" is a select breed who has it in his blood to run, and to run against other horses.

Like his former noble patrons—dukes, earls, barons, knights —he too carries a tag—a certain rating, a certain caste. But unlike the aristocrat, the thoroughbred must prove in action time and again, day after day, that he deserves his tag, or he loses it and gets a lower ranking. From being known as a "duke," he becomes known as a "baron," or even in time as a mere "knight."

So when we run across a "duke" or an "earl" among horses,

we can usually be pretty sure that he has the full measure of quality that goes with the tag!

What is class? Some experts say it is *speed*. But this can't be the whole truth, since classy horses often run their races slower than cheaper horses. It isn't always the classy horse who holds a track record. Other experts say it is *heart* and *courage, consistency,* the ability to run any distance over any kind of footing, packing high weights.

Actually, it is all these things—and something else! That something else is a mystery, a mystery of the blood lines. At any rate, there is nothing that will beat a horse so decisively as racing him with his betters, that is, with horses who have more *class.*

If a horse is not trying, we can certainly pick him as a loser. If a horse is trying hard but is not in his best form, or out of form, we can pick him as a loser. If a horse is trying very hard, and is in the best of form, we can still pick him as a loser—if he is traveling today in rough company, that is, if he is *overmatched.*

The "upper nobility" of the thoroughbred world—the stakes, handicap and quality allowance animals—are mentioned here because a certain segment of the general public is not aware of class even to this extent. This public doesn't usually bet stakes horses against claiming horses, because these two levels seldom get mixed in actual racing. . . . But it would be no exaggeration to say that if they *did* get mixed, you would find an enormous amount of hard cash laid down on the cheapsters. It is a known fact that thousands upon thousands of dollars are blown daily on *cheap claimers* racing against *classy claimers.*

Money is the great yardstick nowadays. When we want to express the quality of a horse, we say he is a $2,000 horse or maybe a $10,000 horse. If he doesn't run in claiming races, where the price is announced, he nevertheless has a price. You can buy him, if he's cheap, for $1,000 or less; and you can buy him, if he's a champion, for $1,000,000, or more.

Fortunately for cheapsters, there are not too many of these "newspaper" horses around, and most of the horses the horseplayer deals with have a market price-range far lower. This book is dedicated not to the princes and dukes of turfdom, who are so few in number, but to the thousands and thousands of mere knights, who make up the bulk of racing programs at all tracks. These horses do not run in stakes races, or get their names in headlines very often, but there is just as much difference in quality among them as among pebbles on the beach.

This question of class, or quality, from one average animal to another, is the most tricky one in the book for the general public to follow. Joe Blow may believe too much in class, thinking of the "newspaper" horses, or he may believe too little in it, thinking that if he, Joe, is as good as the next man (which may be true), then this horse is as good as the next horse (which is strictly false).

As we pointed out in the previous chapter, horses *do* move into and out of form. They get better or they get worse, and sometimes this is a temporary condition with them, and sometimes it isn't. A few horses get better and stay that way. Most of them get worse and stay *that* way. Out of the thousands of two-year-olds who come onto the tracks each year, some of them with very good breeding, only a relative few become "good" animals. As three-year-olds, even fewer remain good. And among four-year-olds there are hardly any really good ones left.

What happens to them? They become the "knights"—the majority of so-so animals, the "in-and outers" who run at *this* claiming price when they are in form, and at *that lower* claiming price when they are sick or sore or out of form.

These animals have therefore what may be called a "variable class." They may run at $10,000 at certain times and $5,000 other times.

Certain of the females of the species, fillies and mares, may not want to run in the spring and summer, when sex rears its ugly head in the equine world. So they seem "out of form" and may descend the class scale as a result. Then, when fall rolls around, and cooler breezes clear the air, they may pay more attention to business and start running again, thus getting *classier* again. Likewise, all horses, like all people, feel better or worse at different times, for various reasons, and become more or less proficient in their work.

Below the level, then, of champion horses, whose class everybody is well acquainted with, there is the great majority of horses whose class it is sometimes hard to figure —so hard for Joe Blow that he becomes economic putty in the invisible hands of the Third Man.

For, if a trainer loves to make his horse appear "out of form" to Joe precisely on the day the animal is to be "sent" for the rubles, then this same trainer can get hysterical with joy at fooling the public about the class of his animal, and thus getting a whopping mutuel price in winning a race.

So the question of deciding whether a horse is overmatched in a given race cannot be answered by a simple rule of thumb. The Third Man is a foxy character, and we must be on our guard when a horse is dropped down in class or stepped up in class. It may be that somebody is about to be robbed. And it *could* be you!

By "dropped down" or "stepped up" we do not mean a mere $500 or $1,000 either way, which is hardly ever a significant class change, except for the cheapest. For a horse worth

$10,000 or more it is not worth noting. In the case of horses worth $15,000 or $20,000, only a class change of at least $5,000 could be considered significant.

You should keep an open mind about class changes that are not too sharp, and remember that most animals rise or fall in value as their form improves or declines.

Keeping in mind the chicanery of trainers on the one hand, and the gullibility and lack of information of the collective public on the other, let's see if we can separate the men from the boys, in terms of class, and tell when the boys are going to take a licking.

How do we go about this? First of all we try to make a shrewd guess as to *"basic class."* Since most animals do not rise very high on the class scale before they fall again, they tend to fluctuate between say a $2,000 status and a $4,000 status; a $5,000 and a $10,000; a $12,000 and a $20,000.

If a horse wins about four out of 20 races in a class of around $5,000, for instance, we can say he is a "solid" $5,000 animal. The same goes for other brackets. This is a rough-and-ready approach and is not intended to be "scientific" in any sense of the word, since few things about horse racing are scientific, contrary to what some people have written on the subject. So, everything we say here is to be understood as "approximate," "more or less," etc.

When a horse does not run in claiming races but in allowance or better company, we must determine his rough class bracket by checking out the other horses in the race, one or more of which usually has been "on the block" in recent times. Then, we must refer to the table, just above the Past Performance record in the *Daily Racing Form* which shows a horse's money winnings last year and so far this year. When we are dealing with no claiming price whatsoever in an animal's record, then money winnings alone serves as our guide.

If a horse wins about one-fifth of his starts in a class range of $5,000-$10,000, he can be considered a pretty good hide for about the $7,500 class. He certainly belongs in that class. If he does better than this, he might be capable of racing at a higher price. If he does worse than this, it may be that he belongs in a cheaper class bracket. The idea is to average his running prices.

Obviously, horses in a given race which have won more money are to be preferred to horses which have won less—unless the lower money winner should have a higher average win per race run. This can be determined by dividing the number of races run into the money won.

If the Past Performance tables do not show the class or claiming bracket a horse was racing in any farther back than a month or two, then we must guess the class by the money won. If there is a good average of money won per race run, the horse may have been running in better company then. And conversely, when the average money was poor, it may be the horse was running in cheaper company at that time.

A little practice in reading over the *Daily Racing Form* or the *Morning Telegraph,* on this point, will make you a pretty good guesser of "basic class."

However, if the basic-class angle were all we had to go on, we would be in sorry shape indeed in the hands of the Third Man. Because, while basic class is something to think about, at all times, when casing a race, it is the animal's present class that is all-important! And right here is where the trainer has a tremendous jump on us. He has been working the animal out in the morning; he knows the horse the way you know your dog.

Before deciding whether a horse is overmatched today, ask yourself the following questions in looking over his recent previous races:

Did he lose or run back *because he was overmatched,* or because:

He was off-form?
He was outrun because of a hot pace?
He was going the wrong distance?
He was not favored by the track, or track condition?

Whenever a horse is stepped-up or dropped-down we must be especially careful about eliminating him from the race. For the general public knows just enough about "class" to lay off horses that are stepping up and to bet horses which are stepping down. And this causes the price on stepped-up animals to go very high sometimes, obscuring the stable betting. It also causes the price on stepped-down animals to go very low sometimes, obscuring the fact that the stable is not betting.

So, whenever we assume that a horse is overmatched we must not rely too much on the Tote Board. It is only when the Tote Board seems to indicate no inside bet and the Past Performances show a weakness in the horse as to Form, Pace, Distance or Footing—that we can safely throw this animal out. If this double-check (which should be made when considering *any* single factor) is not carried out carefully on the Class Factor, we may find ourselves in the same boat as Joe Blow, flat-footed and open-mouthed, as the "cheap stiff" which pays 30-1, comes winging his way home on top of the so-called "class."

Likewise, if we should think a particular horse is undermatched today because of a sharp drop-down, we must not rely too much on the past performances, for this animal may have gone bad suddenly. There is such a thing as the trainer dropping a horse way down, sometimes from $10,000, say, to $2,000, very suddenly, so that the animal may look like a lead-pipe cinch on the past performances. However, if we can detect a lack of stable betting, we should avoid this beast like the plague. For there is no other conclusion possible except that this animal has gone wrong, perhaps seriously so, and the trainer is praying that somebody will claim it and take it off his hands. He has no other intention than this —yet the public will bet thousands on this horse to win the race!

So it is only when you look into the crystal ball from all the angles—*and all at the same time*—that you are safe. And this is doubly true on the Class Angles, for there is more stable monkey-business in this department than in any other.

Use these "class" angles (*but only in connection with other factors*) for spotting well-meant horses and for picking sure-fire losers:

(See chapter 13, chart study B.)

A. If an animal has been running far back in lower claiming or allowance race brackets and is stepping up today, we can pick him as a loser, if the mutuel price today rises *as it should,* and we detect no Tote Board action. *LOSER.*

B. If an animal has been running close up, or winning, in lower claiming or allowance race brackets and is stepping up today, we can pick him as a loser, if the mutuel price today *rises sharply* over those previous races. *LOSER.* If the price does not rise sharply, the animal must be considered. *POSSIBILITY.*

C. If an animal has been running back in higher claiming or allowance race brackets, and is stepping down today, we can pick him as a loser, if the mutuel price today rises over the mutuel price in those previous efforts. *LOSER.* If the mutuel price falls lower, or if we detect Tote action, the animal must be considered. *POSSIBILITY.*

(See chapter 14, examples 2, 3, 5, and 7.)

7. THE PACE THAT KILLS

So FAR, WE HAVE only talked about races—we haven't watched them run. We have been setting up yardsticks for throwing out animals that are not trying, not in their best form, or not able to cope with the company they are pushed into, in a given race. Now, since *time,* or *speed,* is the very guts of all horse racing, we will probably understand this very important factor better if we set up a few simple examples of competition, and run them off—on paper.

In picking losers we must realize that nothing except perhaps a lack of class can be more fatal to an animal's chance of winning than *slow time.* By slow time, we do not necessarily mean *final time*—which is the horse's potential time for the entire race, but slow time at a certain stage of a race.

Let's try to make this clearer by taking two animals out of our stable—Imaginary Stables, Inc.—and run them in a match race. Match races used to be popular years ago, but have since fallen out of favor.

For this example, we will use a *sprint* race.

In order to make everything as equal as possible, we will take two three-year-old colts, both of which are good sprinters, assign them 120 pounds each to carry over six furlongs (three-quarters of a mile). We know they are both in top-notch condition and ready to win. They both like today's fast track. Their names are Cheap Jack and Classy Cliff.

To top it all off, each has a "best time" for the distance of six furlongs in 1:10 (one minute and ten seconds). This time is recent and in both cases was made here at Hypothetical Park, on the same day, in different races.

Now, the only significant difference between these two animals is that Cheap Jack is a good $5,000 claiming plater and Classy Cliff usually runs at around $15,000.

Remember, they both can run the distance in 1:10.

Okay. They're in the gate—and they're off!

Cheap Jack breaks alertly and moves into an early lead, as Classy Cliff trails by two lengths at the furlong pole. Cheap Jack, going in his best form, draws out to a five-length lead at the quarter mile, as Classy Cliff who seems slow to get into stride, begins to run. Cheap Jack, going nicely on top, approaches the half-mile as Classy Cliff begins rapidly to close the gap, and as they move into the stretch, they are neck and neck. The race is fought down into mid-stretch, when suddenly Classy Cliff pulls ahead, increases his winning margin with every step, to win going away by five lengths.

His winning time is one minute and ten seconds (1:10)— just what he figured to run it in! But what about Cheap Jack? He was beaten by five lengths. His time was 1:11. And he is capable of 1:10. What happened to him?

Well, he had no excuse. Nor did Joe Blow, if he happened to buy a ticket on the animal just because the odds were high.

Cheap Jack was beaten because he was *overmatched*. Even Joe knows that, but neither Joe nor the general public can tell you *how* it happened. They might say, "Oh well, class will tell," and go on the next race. But it is very important to know how it happened. Because it happens every day on the race track, when the class difference is not nearly so wide.

The secret of Cheap Jack's defeat lies in the "pace times," the fractional times, of the two horses. Here they are:

	¼ (QUARTER)	½ (HALF)	¾ (FINISH)	FINAL TIME
Cheap Jack	22 seconds	23	26	1:11
Classy Cliff	23 seconds	23	24	1:10

Classy Cliff ran an even race, a steady race, almost the same speed all the way. Cheap Jack's race was very uneven. He had blazing speed for the first quarter, cooled off somewhat in the second quarter, and flattened out completely in the final quarter. Why did he flatten out? Because he was *challenged*. When he couldn't meet the challenge, he lost heart, and so did his jockey, perhaps.

Cheap Jack, you will note, ran the half mile in 45 seconds, and that is really flying. In his own class, he could have outrun his competition, pulled off after the half mile, and won, *still flying* in 1:10. But, as you see, he couldn't get away from Classy Cliff.

This is a very simple example, and perhaps too simple, but it makes the point we wish to underscore, namely, that *speed has worth only in the class in which it is made.* It is relative to this class and has no absolute value. Horses win races at slower or faster times, according to the company, or according to the pace times of a given race.

Good horses running with cheapsters will usually run fast enough to win. Whatever it takes to win, they deliver it. If they have to run six furlongs in 1:10, they'll do it; if they have to run it in 1:09, they'll do that too. Good horses stay near enough to the pace-setters to catch them somewhere along the line. Cheap horses either can't stay near the pace, and lose the race at the outset, or they may set the pace, and be unable to finish anywhere but "up the track."

Now, this matter of pace time is important not only when a good horse meets a cheap horse, but also when a cheap horse meets another cheap horse. Because each cheap horse is different. One has blinding early speed, but no late speed. Another has no early speed, but good late speed. Still another tends to turn in an evenly-run race every time.

A moment's thought will tell you that the effect of matching such horses in various races will cause each race to be run differently as to pace times and thus have a great bearing on the outcome.

As an example, if Cheap Jack meets another animal just like himself—call her Cheap Jill—they may both go out on top and set such a blazing pace as to knock each other out by the time they reach the stretch, and so allow old Johnny-Come Lately, a slow-starting, but fast-closing animal, to come down on the front end!

However, if Cheap Jack is the only early-speed animal in a cheap race (let's say Cheap Jill is scratched), then it may very well be that Larry Long, an animal who needs distance, and Steady Steve, an animal that requires a slow half-mile pace to get into contention, won't have much of a chance. Neither will Slow Moe or Sam the Stiff. They will have to wait for another day—a day when Cheap Jack goes out of form, starts on his down-cycle, loses his early speed. Then they will beat him, for it will be a different kind of race.

Roy the Router, a distance horse, will win at six furlongs when Pan Flash and Sometimes Sue "drop dead" in the stretch and run that final quarter in something like 30 seconds, after setting a hot early pace. And Steady Steve will come into his own on that day when Morning Glory, Throat Latcher and Betting Tool wear one another down before they hit the stretch turn.

The point we want to make is this: *"How* will the race be run?"

We must look into the crystal ball, by checking the past performances, to get an idea of how the *pace pattern* will shape up. If it shapes up as a blazing pace, then certain animals won't be able to keep up and may lose all chance at the outset. If it shapes up as a moderate pace, then certain steady, or come-from-behind animals will have a chance. If it's going to be a slow pace, then the worst kind of beetle might jump up and surprise you with the way he can *run,* when he is not *outrun.* Even Sam the Stiff might win this kind of a race.

Just above the past performance charts in *Daily Racing Form,* there is a very important table which shows the "best time" at the distance of each horse in the race. If the animal has gone this distance in recent times, this table shows not only his time but the weight carried then, the weight carried today, and the date and track condition of the race, and the oval on which it was run.

This information is very valuable, if you use it properly. It is very dangerous to your bankroll if you use it carelessly. This "best time" of a horse might be called his "potential" or "basic" time. It is something to think about, but *it is not enough.* For, as in the case of class, it is not his speed at *that time* or in *that spot* which is decisive—but his speed right now, his current speed, in *this* spot!

(The real usefulness of this "best time" table comes when we try to gauge an animal's "best distance," which we will take up in the next chapter, and in judging and comparing the ability of horses coming from various tracks.)

However, since we are interested in picking the losers, not the winner, this "basic time" gives us at least one valuable reverse angle. In the case of an animal that has been running a certain distance, over and over, and has *never* come up with a good final time—we can conclude that he is a pretty slow beast and not likely to win today, or any other day, for that matter. And, we can eliminate him from our calculations.

The "best time" factor is also helpful in shedding light on the animal's time-weight ratio. If a horse has carried 120 pounds say, over a certain distance with comparatively good time, and today he is packing only 100 pounds—then, *other things being equal,* he might be dangerous today. And vice-versa, if he carried 110 pounds at the distance, with comparatively *bad* time, and is toting 120 today—then he might very well be a loser today, and we can pick him as such.

It is always a smart idea to play "District Attorney" with an animal and cross-question his time-weight ratio. You might catch him in a lie!

In the case of an animal which has been out of form (really), but lately has been showing unmistakable signs of returning to condition—good workouts, early speed in races that are improving, or sudden, stout late speed—it might mean that he is returning to his "best time." And if that "best time" is speedy, relative to the other horses in today's race—then we must proceed with great caution. This beast may be THE winner. . . . And the worst mistake we can make, in *our* strategy, is to pick such a horse as a loser!

This animal may have been beaten two lengths the other day by another horse in today's race, but if he has a better "basic time" and is now moving towards it by leaps and bounds, as improving animals do, then he *could* turn the tables today and beat *that* animal by two lengths.

Here, then, is the place to talk about the puzzling question of beaten lengths. For, as we pointed out in the chapter on Form, not only Joe Blow, but most public handicappers, who *should* know better, make a religion out of turning thumbs down on a horse which has been running rather far back in his recent previous races. The public cannot or will not realize that in very many cases, the number of lengths a horse gets beat by means absolutely nothing at all. . . . It may be that a horse has speed and quality, just as well when he runs *last* as when he runs *first!* If the animal is "driving" (trying and under pressure from the jockey) down to the finish pole, then all we have to do to calculate his speed is to add ⅕ of a second for each length he is beaten by the winner. This is true, no matter what his final finish position happens to be.

If the final time of the race is 1:11 and this animal finishes sixth or seventh, beaten ten lengths—then his time was 1:13. . . . This might be good time for another race, another pace pattern, another set of conditions. Let's say this animal, Sad Sack, is going today in a race that will be run in 1:13. Does he figure, other things being equal? Of course he does, right on top!

The great confusion about beaten lengths comes from the ignorance of the public on the question of whether a horse was "driving" home or not. Joe Blow looks at the past performance charts and shudders whenever he sees an animal that was beaten 20 lengths last time out. . . . And then, when this same animal wins today's race, going away, by five lengths, he wants to tear up his program and scream that the races are as "crooked as a spiral staircase." The feeling is understandable, but the hard truth of the matter is that very few races are ever rigged.

Joe doesn't realize that, in many cases, where a horse is beaten by 20 lengths, this defeat does not represent the horse's best effort at all. The animal was probably outrun and the jockey eased him up. There is no percentage in whipping a dead horse.

In this chapter we have been talking about races at Six Furlongs, the most popular sprint distance—but the principles are much the same at any distance. In the next chapter we will deal with the question of final times and pace patterns at shorter and longer distances.

So, let's ask a few pointed questions about speed. Like everything else in racing, it is a *relative* thing—relative to the other factors. So, before we decide that a horse is too slow to win today's race, we must answer the following:

Was the animal losing or running back in his recent previous races, *because he was too slow,* or because:

> *He was off-form*
> *He was overmatched*
> *He was going the wrong distance*
> *He was not favored by the track or track condition?*

If this doesn't help us, then we must go further. To the pace-time question. *Was he outrun in his recent previous races, and will he be outrun today?*

How can we visualize the pace pattern of today's race if we do not have available the pace times of the horses in their past performances? The past performance records of *The Morning Telegraph* provide this information (for what it is worth) but those of *Daily Racing Form* do not.

Fortunately, in our strategy, we do not have to rely on split-second figures. A lot of bosh, usually labelled "scientific," has been written on this subject, and all kinds of charts, tables, rules—and even slide rules, have been offered for sale to the guillible horseplayer.

Instead of using a slide-rule we simply use our head. We look over the past performances of the animals in today's race to see how they achieved their recent final times. Did they achieve the final times by *driving all the way,* by *driving just part of the way, or by not driving at all,* having been "left" at the beginning and not thereafter persevering.

If you look at the charts for this *one thing*—for a minute

or two—you will begin to see a pattern. It is like looking into the crystal ball to see how the race will be run. By comparing recent final times and the way the animals achieved them, you will get a pretty fair idea of who can keep up today and who can't—who will be able to stay on the pace and who will not. Who can come from behind in time —and who can't. Who will stop, and who will fight all the way.

Every race is different. When a horse finds that he can *keep up* he will run a much better race than when he is clobbered out of contention in the very beginning. And when he can keep up, his jockey will dig into him to get the very best out of him—because *whenever you can keep up, you have a chance*—and you may be THE winner. Today is always a new day, and today's spot is always a new spot— *perhaps a slower pace.* But when you can't keep up, why knock yourself out! It is always better, in horse racing, if you are going to lose—to lose by a country mile! *Because it sweetens the odds for the next try!*

(*See chapter 13, chart study C.*)

Use these "time and pace" angles (*but only in connection with other factors*) for spotting well-meant horses and for picking sure-fire losers:

A. If an animal has been winning or running close up, with relatively slow final time, we can pick him as a loser today, if the mutuel price today is higher than in the previous effort, or efforts, or if we detect no inside betting. *LOSER.*

B. If an animal has been losing or running back, while "driving" (that is, under pressure) all the way—and we calculate his time as relatively "good" (by adding ⅕ of a second for each beaten length), we cannot automatically pick him as a loser, especially if the mutuel price today is lower than in the previous effort or efforts. *POSSIBILITY.*

. . . If we calculate his time as relatively "slow," we can pick him as a *loser*, especially if the mutuel price is higher today, or if we detect no inside betting. *LOSER*.

C. If an animal has been running back while "driving" only part of the way (having been eased up), then we cannot automatically pick him as a loser. If he has good basic time for the distance, and if the mutuel price is lower than in the previous effort, or efforts, then he must be considered. *POSSIBILITY*. . . . If he does not have good basic time for the distance, and if the mutuel price is higher than previously, we can pick him as a loser. *LOSER*.

D. If an animal has been running back, while not "driving" at any stage of the race, having been outrun at the outset, and eased up by the jockey, we cannot automatically pick him as a loser. This is especially true if he has a good time for the distance and if the mutuel price today is lower than in the previous effort, or efforts. *POSSIBILITY*. . . . If the animal has poor or relatively slow basic time for the distance, and if this "far back" running is characteristic of the animal—then we can pick him as a loser, regardless of the mutuel price. *LOSER*.

E. If an animal has been winning or running close up in his recent races, with good final time, then we cannot pick him as a loser, if there is Tote action on the horse. It is possible for the price on such an animal to rise over the previous effort, or efforts (when the public jumps on some other animal as the emotional favorite). Nevertheless, this horse should always be considered. *POSSIBILITY*.

(*See chapter 14, examples 4, 6, and 9.*)

8. THE DISTANCE OF DEFEAT

IN PROFESSIONAL BASEBALL, an outfielder is not expected to play the infield positions. A good left-fielder is not called upon suddenly to become a shortstop. Nor is a first baseman required to be also a catcher, or a third baseman. There are a few all-around ball players, of course, who can step in and play any position, but they are few in number.

Ball players become specialists. By natural talent and by practice, in a given position, they become very skillful. A center-fielder, if he were suddenly put at third base, would not turn in the kind of job a regular third baseman would, and might make enough errors to lose the game for his team. He might be a topnotch ball player but he would be competing in an unsuitable spot. And he would look bad.

So it is with professional race horses. By a combination of natural endowments and experience, they become specialists at this distance or at that distance. A few of them, the very good and useful ones, might be able to compete at any distance, but these are not numerous.

When a good specialist sprinter, in sharp shape, is sent out at a mile or more against his own kind, who are routers, he will almost surely be defeated, even if he leads the race down to the middle of the stretch. And a good specialist router, sent at a sprint distance with his own kind, will almost never get up in time to win the race, although he might close with blazing speed and pass tired horses in the stretch.

We have all seen this in playing the races. It seems to be just what you would expect. The sprinter goes out on top and then stops. The router closes with a rush but doesn't get there.

However, what baffles the general public, and Joe Blow, who read the form sheet in a superficial manner, is this:

Very often a good sprinter, going a route, *doesn't even show early speed*. He never gets into contention at any stage of the race. And very often a good front-running router *doesn't even show late speed*, in a sprint race. This makes Joe very angry, when he has bet such an animal on the hope of bringing one down at a long price. He is angry because he lost his money, of course, but he is also angry because the horse didn't even turn in a decent *losing* effort.

Very often Joe, and the collective public, will bet a sprinter to Place in a route race on the theory that he will quit but at the same time hang on for second. And he will bet a long-shot router in a sprint race, to Show, say, on the theory that while the beast may not get to the front end, he will close fast enough to be third.

Of all the foolish ways the collective public will throw away its money, this is the classic way, next to betting cheap horses against class horses.

While it may happen once in a long while for a sprinter to turn in a good effort at a route, or a router to sparkle in a sprint race, the truth of the matter is that such an animal, in such a race, does not figure to show any kind of decent effort whatever—neither early speed nor late speed. Not any kind of speed at all!

Why is this? It is because of the pace times, the fractional times. It is true that a sprinter *could* go out on top in a route race—but if he's really trying to win his jockey won't allow it. The jockey lays off the pace and tries to reserve and rate his animal—but what happens then? When he calls on the animal to run after they have passed the six furlong pole, the beast won't do it. He has already run as far as he wants to, reserved, rated or what have you? So he stops, despite everything, without having shown anything at all. . . . In the case of the router going a sprint distance, the jockey, if he's trying to win, will hustle the beast for dear life for the half mile, to try to get into contention. He hardly ever does get into contention, and even when he does, his horse is then pooped, from such unfamiliar hustling tactics, and stops dead. So, it's not so easy to make a specialist perform well outside his specialty.

If this is true, then why does the public remain convinced that such misplaced animals have a chance—even to be in the money? It must be that Joe Blow has collected a bet somewhere by playing such an animal.

Well, he has, but he doesn't know why! . . . He collected a bet one day when a six-furlong horse was *dropped down in class*, sharply, and sent out at a mile and one eighth—a distance that seemed very improbable for him. . . . Or when a classy router was dropped down sharply and sent at five or six furlongs against cheapsters. The drop-down in class is the factor which changed the picture.

It is hard enough for such a horse to win at an unsuitable distance, but it does happen once in a while, just as a Big League shortstop might go down into the bush leagues and successfully play any position, infield or outfield, better than the bush-league players around him.

With horses, it is a matter of pace times, again, fractional times that are slow or speedy. A classy horse is used to fierce pace times, so that when he finds himself on a soft pace, he does unexpected things. He gets up in a sprint race, or he goes on in a route race.

We mention the exceptions because we want to prove the rule.

Now, so far, we have made it too simple. For it is not merely sprinter against router that we have to deal with, but a whole variety of distance abilities in horses as distinct as the positions on a ball team, where each man *plays best* in his *best position.* We might classify our equine athletes as follows, not scientifically, but very roughly:

The Short Sprinter	(Five furlongs to six)
The Sprinter	(Six furlongs to six and one-half)
The Long Sprinter	(Six and one-half to seven)
The Middle Runner	(Seven furlongs to one mile)
The Short Router	(One mile to one mile and one-sixteenth)
The Router	(One mile and one-sixteenth to one mile and one-quarter)
The Long Router	(One mile and one-quarter to two miles)

You will find that horses have a *best distance* and that when they go this distance they are dangerous. What they have in the way of speed and endurance finds its very best expression under these conditions. But *even an extra half furlong*, one way or another can upset them when they are going the wrong distance. Other things being equal, this is the Distance of Defeat!

If this is true, why then does a trainer run a horse at a wrong distance? Well, for several reasons. When he is not really trying, a trainer uses a switch in distances for conditioning an animal, or for *pointing* an animal for a future race.

As we said earlier, a sprinter may show signs of stopping in a sprint race. By running him a farther distance a few times you may build up his staying ability for the sprint. And you might pep up a router and stimulate early speed in him by running him a few times in a sprint race. But above all, you can *manipulate* a horse—cause him to lose—by merely placing him in such a wrong spot. You can do this without saying a word to a jockey or anybody else—and there will be no risk of bringing the stewards down on your tail. After all, if a trainer is stupid and enters the horse in the wrong kind of a race that's his business. This is the official way of looking at it. And the same thing applies to running a horse over his head, in too classy company.

However, very often, the Third Man is really trying when he puts the horse in at a strange distance. He really feels that his Sprinter, which is in hot shape, can go out and win at a middle distance, say. And besides he figures to get a juicy mutuel if he can do it. Whereas, at six furlongs, he might get only 2-1, or 3-1. Big mutuel odds always wield a strong influence over the good judgement of the Third Man, who is only human, and therefore allows his emotions to override his common sense.

That is why, as we said before, it is not good enough to know that an animal is trying. As successful horseplayers we must know this and one more thing—can he do it?

While the trainer sometimes makes mistakes about the ability of his horse to run well at a strange distance, and thus loses his own money and the money of the insiders by wagering on the animal—more often than not *he knows what he is doing* by switching distance. He is fooling the public!

He is going into his bag of tricks to win a race where the

public handicappers think he can't do it. Public handicappers have a short memory, and if a horse has not been going a route for some time, they forget that the animal *is* a router. Or vice-versa. It is then that the Third Man pulls a rabbit out of the hat.

We have to protect ourselves against this sort of thing by never assuming that just because a horse has been running in sprint races recently that he can't go at a mile or more. Or because he has been running routes that he can't get up at six furlongs. For, it may be that the distance he is going today is his *best* distance—despite the fact he has not been running it!

So, we have to check carefully the table at the top of the past performance charts which shows the "best time at the distance" of the horses in the race. As we said in the previous chapter this table is very valuable in pointing up what may be an animal's *best distance*. But, it is even more valuable in revealing the Distance of Defeat.

For, this table shows us the "best time" the horse has achieved in previous races at this distance. That is to say, the animal may have gone this distance 10 or 20 times, in this class and in that, on this pace time and on that, at this track or at that track—and *here* is the *best* he has ever done. . . . Now, it is clear that if a horse has gone the distance a number of times and has never come up with a better time than some of the other horses in today's race—it is not likely that he will suddenly outdo himself today, and break his own record.

This kind of animal we can pick as a loser!

On the other hand if the table shows us that a horse has, at one time or another, run this particular distance in very sharp time, even though it was at another track, and perhaps quite a while back, we must be very careful about picking him as a loser today. Especially if he has been running at another distance in his most recent previous races. Today he may finally be sent at his *best distance,* and what looked liked a *lack of form* last week will be proved today to have been *a wrong distance.* Either a training maneuver or a manipulation.

However, we must never assume that because a horse can win at six furlongs, say, that he can win at six-and-one-half furlongs. Even though we classify both these distances as "sprint" distances, it simply isn't true that every horse, or even most horses, can run them equally well. The same thing applies between six-and-one-half furlongs and seven furlongs; between seven furlongs and one mile; between one-mile-and-one-sixteenth and one-mile-and one-eighth. Where the distance switch is slight, we can "handicap the trainer" better than when it is sharp. In the former case he is usually *trying.*

But, as we said before an extra half furlong, one way or another, can upset the animal. It may well "break his back," or it will keep him from getting up in time. Always remember that this specialization has gone a long way in modern horse racing—so far, in fact, that there are some horses who can win at only *one* distance. Even 70 yards, more or less, would defeat them! There are many horses running at half-mile "bull-ring" tracks that can race at five furlongs, in a brilliant manner, but couldn't go six furlongs to save their lives. This is what condemns them to the cheap half-mile tracks. For at big tracks there are very few races at such a short distance, for older horses.

One of the most common mistakes in reading the past performances is to seize on a horse, who closes fast but never gets there, as a horse who will surely win if given more distance. Now, in some cases this is true, but it is very often false. There is a type of Sprint horse who always closes with good speed, passing tired horses in the stretch, but which himself won't go farther than six furlongs. What looks like a need for distance is merely *late sprint speed*.

The opposite error is to seize on a front-running horse in a route race as a horse who will surely win if dropped down in distance to a sprint race. This is usually false reasoning because of the slowish pace times in route races where many of the animals are being *rated* by the jockeys.

Perhaps the greatest confusion of all exists among those superficial form players who talk about "quitters" among horses. They see where a horse got out on top and then stopped, and they assume he is a "quitter." They make this assumption without reference to the pace times, or to the form cycle. Horses which are coming into form often stop the first or second try, before going on to a win. There *is* such a thing as a "quitter," a faint hearted beast—but this is an animal who shows a record of *nothing but* quitting, under any and all circumstances. Such an animal, of course, we can pick as a loser, any day. With these others—that is, most animals—we must be careful.

Now, even when a horse is going his best distance he can look like he is unsuited to the distance if he happens to be overmatched, or out of form, or going on an unsuitable track. And even when a horse is going a wrong distance, he can look better than he really is if he happens to be undermatched, in sharp shape or going on footing that is especially to his liking, say, a sloppy or muddy track.

So, before we decide that a horse is unsuited to the distance today, we must look at his recent races.

Was the animal losing or running back *because he was going the wrong distance,* or because:

> *He was off-form?*
> *He was overmatched?*
> *He was outrun because of a hot pace?*

He was not favored by the track or track condition?

This kind of checking should be made in connection with the table of "best times" to determine whether a horse is going a wrong distance today. If the table shows *no time* for the distance for the animal, then he has not gone this distance in recent times—and perhaps for a good reason, namely that the trainer knows he is not good at this distance. In the case of older horses, who have been racing a year or two, this is pretty good reasoning—enough in fact to suspect the horse as a loser. It should never be used on younger horses. For who knows what an untried animal can or cannot do!

Use the following "distance" angles (but only in connection with other factors) for spotting well-meant horses and for picking sure-fire loser:

(*See chapter 13, chart studies C and D.*)

A. If an animal which has been going a certain distance, and losing or running back, is today going the same distance and has a comparatively poor time for this distance, we can pick him as a loser, if there is no evidence of inside betting. *LOSER*. . . . If he has a comparatively good time for this distance, he must be considered, especially if the mutuel price is lower than in those previous races, or if there is evidence of stable betting. *POSSIBILITY*.

B. If an animal which has been going a certain distance, and losing or running back, is today switching to a distance for which he has comparatively poor "best time," we can pick him as a loser, if there is a lack of Tote action. *LOSER*. . . . If he is switching to a distance for which he has comparatively good "best time," he must be considered, especially if we can detect inside betting. *POSSIBILITY*.

C. If an animal which has been going a certain distance and winning, or running close up, is today switching to a distance for which he has comparatively poor "best time," we can pick him as a loser, if there is a lack of Tote action. *LOSER*. If he has comparatively good "best time," he must be considered, especially when we can detect inside betting. *POSSIBILITY*.

(See chapter 14, examples 5, 7, and 9.)

9. GROUNDS FOR SURPRISE

If ALL RACE TRACKS were the same size and shape, and the quality of the soil were indentical, it would be less of a problem to compare the ability of horses in a given race that are coming from different ovals. But, each track is somewhat different. One has sharper turns, longer stretches, harder or softer footing than others. These things have a great deal to do with the variation in time the same animal will register in running the same distance at two different tracks.

On a straightaway course, such as the Widener Course at Belmont Park (no longer in use), a horse may run six furlongs a full five seconds faster than he can run the same six furlongs at a half-mile track, where he will have to take the curves a number of times—or perhaps two full seconds faster than he can run the same distance on a mile course. Or, his time may vary a full second or more, from one mile track to another mile track.

Apart from the question of the bends, there is also the matter of cuppy soil, at one track, which holds a horse back, even though it is kind to his legs; and hard soil, at another track, which allows an animal to really scoot, if he likes that sort of footing.

The difference in the hardness or softness of the footing, from one track to another, is in a lesser degree the same difference you get on a given track when it is called "fast" or "slow."

Nowadays there seems to be a great desire on the part of many track managements to "speed up" their respective tracks by "skinning" the surface, which will do the trick.

At any rate, in picking losers, we must be alert to the difference in the way a certain animal will perform from one track to another, or on the same track when it gets "sloppy," "slow," "muddy," "heavy," or "good." These are the official designations which are posted on the Tote Board when a track is "off" because of rain.

Both *Daily Racing Form* and the *Morning Telegraph* use the familiar "X" after a horse's name in the entries to indicate a "mudder."

Horses which have been raced a sufficient number of times will generally reveal whether or not they have a liking for soft or heavy footing, as well as for grass courses, that is, turf racing. Certain animals, needless to say, will improve "five or ten lengths" on an off track. Running way back just the other day, they jump up and win today in the soggy footing. Next time out, on a fast track, they will revert to their old losing ways.

At least, that's the way it seems. Actually it is never quite this simple—except to Joe Blow and about 90% of the public who jump aboard "the mudders" with reckless abandon every time it rains. Just the way they jump aboard "the hot horse," or "the classy horse," or "the speed horse," or "the route horse," etc., on other occasions.

Which is to say that they jump aboard *part of the truth,* but not the truth. In short, a horse does not win just because he is a mudder. He wins because he is a mudder and because of several other things.

A mudder when he goes out on a muddy track, in order to

win, must be in *fair* shape, and not overmatched, and going a suitable distance. Otherwise he will probably lose just as he would if the track were fast. For, remember that mudders win races not by running fast but by running "less slowly" than the others. Just because he "likes" the track, he doesn't become a superior animal able to work wonders. Another beast who "likes" the track less, but the distance more, might cop the race.

The point we want to make here is that there are many degrees of liking and disliking an off track, on the part of a horse, apart from the arbitrary marks indicating a "superior," "good," or "fair" mud runner. Just as there are many degrees of softness or hardness of a track, apart from the official designations of "sloppy," "slow," "muddy," "heavy," or "good."

It may seem that we are getting too technical at this point, and trying to fracture a hair—but the fact *is* that on this question of the variation of time, from one track to another, and at the same track, from *day to day*, along with the question of whether an animal can run on an off track—there is more confusion and ignorance in the public mind than on any other subject in racing. Joe Blow and the collective public hardly ever go beyond the "mud marks" to find a mudder, or beyond the official sign on the Tote Board to determine just what the footing condition is today. And, it would be safe to say, the mud marks and the official signs are wrong, at least half the time.

Since horse-playing is a battle of wits, and the object is to outwit the opponent—then here is an opportunity to get in some tremendous licks!

From the standpoint of picking loser, it works this way:

(1) If the past performances of an animal show fast times, earned at a *race track where fast times mean nothing, because* it is a *speedy track*, and this animal today is switching to

a race track that has slow times, because it is *not* a speedy track—then it may be that this animal does not figure, despite all appearances, and we can pick him as a loser. Or, vice versa, if he is coming from a slowish track to a speedy track, he will look worse than he is—in fact, may be a live contender and this knowledge will enable us to pick certain other horses as losers, despite their seeming "speed."

(2) Many horses who have mud marks do not perform well in the mud. They earned the mud mark at a time when they did perform well, perhaps, but that was some time ago. Right now they are not mudders, but the mark stays on them. Many other horses with mud marks do not perform well in the mud because they are out of form, overmatched, going the wrong distance, etc. . . . All these we can pick as losers when the track is off. Some animals, who have no mud mark, will run brilliantly in the mud—and these we must beware of picking as losers, if they figure in other ways.

(3) After a rain, or repeated rains, a race track normally will go from "sloppy" to "slow" (perhaps to "muddy" or "heavy") and then will start to dry out, so as to be then designated as "good." The track is always undergoing a process of change, from softness to hardness, or vice versa. The official sign on the Tote Board is the roughest kind of guess as to the true state of affairs. It is only after the running times of the races reveal the true condition of the track that the sign changes. *Meanwhile, the public is betting on the basis of misleading information.* We can avoid this costly mistake by knowing how to determine just what the track condition really is. This is very important for picking losers.

How do we go about determining which tracks are speedy and which are not? *Daily Racing Form*, from time to time, includes in certain issues a "Table of Comparative Track

Records," which shows the more or less current track records at various distances on the major tracks. This can be very helpful when considered in connection with a horse's recent time at a certain oval and in connection with a horse's "best time at the distance," as dealt with in the previous chapter. However, this table has its limitations. A track record is one thing, and the average daily speed of average horses is another.

A far better way of checking up on a track is to flip through your racing paper to see if the horses are still running at that particular track. If they are, then it is no problem to determine what the average times for the various distances are adding up to—in this class division and in that. So, if $4,000 horses are running six furlongs there in 1:09, say, and the $4,000 horses here at our track are doing it in only 1:11— then, it is clear, *this animal is not the speedster he might seem to be, on the surface.* . . . It is always a good idea for a horse-player to save back numbers of his racing paper for this kind of checking.

How do we account for the fact that certain horses with mud marks seem to have no liking for the mud, at least at the present time; while others that have no mud marks seem to eat it up? . . . This is a complex question, because as we explained before, the good or bad performance of an animal depends upon other things besides an off track. A horse's physical condition (and we daresay his psychological condition too) changes from time to time (the old gray mare ain't what she used to be). Some people who used to like spinach can't stand the sight of it. Others develop a taste for it. Maybe that's the answer. At any rate, for our purpose, it is enough to warn us to go beyond the mud mark, or the lack of it, to the past performances, where we may be able to *see the evidence,* one way or the other, of the animal's present likes and dislikes. *Also when a horse is in good form, he may run on footing he would otherwise refuse.*

How can we ascertain the true slowness or fastness of a track, over and beyond the official sign on the Tote Board? . . . There is only one certain way. You must develop the habit of writing down the time of each race on your program as soon as it is posted. Then you will never have to worry about arbitrary definitions of the track condition. You will be able to compare today's track, at this particular post time, with yesterday's fast track, and know the track is "one second off" or "two seconds off" or "three seconds off," etc.

This knowledge is very useful, for a "good" track is about one second off, and a "muddy" track about three seconds off. A true "heavy" track is four seconds or more off. A "sloppy" track is about the same speed as a "fast" track, although there are some horses who don't like it, and refuse to run on it.

While we are dealing with tracks and track conditions, it will be well to point out that there is an "unwritten law" of the turf, which track stewards seem to accept without cross-questioning the trainer. It is this: *a horse who is starting at a given track for the first time this meeting is "allowed a race."* What this means, translated into ordinary language, is that the trainer doesn't have to try the first time out if he doesn't care to. . . . So, when the Third Man ships a horse from one track to another, he can dog the animal that first outing (if he doesn't like the mutuel price) and get away with it, even if the beast happens to be the public choice. Then, the second time out (with a nice fat mutuel) he can send the horse for the top spot with a reversal of form that will knock your eye out!

The official track apology to the public for such a dastardly deed on the part of the trainer is that the horse needed one race at the new track to "get the feel of the track" or as "a conditioner," etc. However, the track seldom makes apologies for anything.

This first-time out indulgence on the part of track stewards applies also, of course, to first-time starters and to horses coming out for the first time this meeting. When we are dealing with two-year-olds, who are supposed always to be "green" racers, the track stewards are lenient at all times, first start or fifth start. The explanation here is that these baby racers are "unpredictable." They certainly *are* unpredictable, but when the Third Man gets done manipulating them for a price, there is nothing under the sun more erratic.

We bring up this "unwritten law" because we want to emphasize that there is one type of situation, at least, in horse racing, wherein the trainer can commit bloody murder (of the public bankroll) and get away with it. Needless to say, most trainers take full advantage of such a loophole in the law.

So, a smart horse-player ought to be way up on his toes, with his ears wide open for the Voice of the Tote Board in the case of a horse that showed good form at one track, then showed a dismal first effort at this race track. For the second effort here, especially if the price is right, may be the winging victory.

When we are dealing with first-time starters, or with first-time-outers this meeting, or at this track, we must be very careful, especially on that second try, which may be accompanied by a shift up or down in class and a whopping stable bet.

Another trainer's trick is to use an off track as an excuse for an animal's bad performance when the odds are low. He can always explain to the stewards, if called upon, that the animal doesn't like the mud right now. Or, if he wins on an off track, when it appears to the public that the beast dislikes the mud, the trainer can always say that he, too, was taken by surprise—"in fact, didn't bet a nickle." Trainers are highly skilled in lying to stewards, and because racing is so uncertain anyway, the stewards don't know what to believe.

Before we decide that a horse dislikes today's off track or is not favored by the track itself, we must look at the past performances and ask the following questions:

Was the animal losing or running back *because he was not favored by the track or track condition,* or because:

> *He was off-form?*
> *He was overmatched?*
> *He was outrun because of a hot pace?*
> *He was going the wrong distance?*

There is one more thing we should say about tracks. Some of them are cheap and some of them are classy, just like the horses who usually race there. So that horses coming from classy tracks (usually big-city tracks) are always tougher than horses coming from cheap tracks (usually small-town ones), even though the latter have been running at the same class figure, and have Speed Ratings just as high. For Speed Ratings* cannot be trusted in comparing horses coming from different ovals, and they are downright meaningless in comparing horses who have been running at different distances.

As a matter of fact, we believe that Speed Ratings are very misleading at all times and that a horse-player will do better if he doesn't use them at all. To figure how fast a horse is running *in terms of minutes and seconds* is the familiar way,

---

* The *Daily Racing Form* explains its Speed Ratings this way:

Speed ratings appearing in past performances are based on a comparison of each horse's running time with the track record existing at the beginning of the meeting. The track record will receive a standard rating of 100—thus, a horse equaling the record will have a speed rating of 100. For each one-fifth second slower than the track record, one point is deducted. Therefore,

and if the familiar way is correct, then the familiar way is easier and better.

Use the following "track" angles (*but only in connection with other factors*) for spotting well-meant horses and for picking sure-fire losers:

(See chapter 13, chart study D.)

A. If an animal that seems to dislike a certain type of off-track is today going on that type of off-track, and we can detect no inside bet, we can pick him as a loser. *LOSER.*

B. If an animal that seems to like a certain type of off-track is going today on that type of footing, we cannot automatically pick him as a loser, if we detect inside betting. *POSSIBILITY.* However, if there is a marked absence of such betting, we can throw him out. *LOSER.*

C. If an animal that has been running badly on off-tracks is going on a fast track, or perhaps a sloppy track, we cannot automatically pick him as a loser, if we detect stable betting. *POSSIBILITY.* However, if there is no Tote action, we can pick him as a loser. *LOSER.*

---

the rating for a horse running his race two and one-fifth seconds slower than the track record receives a speed rating of 89 (100 minus 11)

EXAMPLE		
Track record	1:10	Rating figure 100
Winner's time	1:10 ⅕	99
Time of Second Horse	1:10 ⅗	97
Time of Third Horse	1:11	95
Time of Fourth Horse	1:11 ⅖	93
Time of Fifth Horse	1:11 ⅘	91

One point (the equivalent of one-fifth second) is deducted from the rating for each length the horse is beaten. Thus, a horse beaten four lengths in a six-furlong race run in 1:11 (rating of 100 where the track record is 1:10) is timed in 1:11 ⅘, receiving a speed rating of 91.

D. If an animal is switching tracks today, or making his first start of the meeting, or his first start of the season or the year, we cannot automatically pick him as a loser, unless we detect a marked absence of inside betting. *LOSER.* When we do detect inside betting, and can tie this up with workouts indicating that the animal is in good shape, we must consider him. And this is especially true if it happens to be the animal's second start, the first try having been a losing effort, and the mutuel price today is lower than in the first start. *POSSIBILITY.*

E. If an animal is switching tracks today, and coming from a "slowish" track to a "speedy" track, we cannot automatically pick him as a loser, especially if we detect inside betting. *POSSIBILITY.* However, when the reserve is true—a "speedy" track to a "slowish" track, we can pick the animal as a loser if we detect no Tote Board action. *LOSER.*

(See chapter 14, examples 5, 6, 8 and 9.)

10. THE LOSING SPOT

THE TIME HAS now come when we must go beyond picking sure-fire losers—a thing we should be able to do by now—and begin picking a few well-meant losers.

With the sure-fire losers out of the way, the race will be narrowed down to the *possible* contenders. Just how many such contenders we will have to deal with naturally depends on the race. In some races, it may be no more than three or four, while in other races, it may be almost every horse in the line-up.

Remember, in our strategy, we are not looking for *the* winner but only for the *actual* contenders—those among the *possible* contenders who figure to be there or thereabouts at the finish. So we never even try to eliminate from a race all but one horse, for this would be just another way of trying to pick *the* winner.

It is not only the hardest thing in the world to pick *the* winner of a horse race, it is not even smart! *More money can be made on the races, more longshots brought down and more winning tickets cashed by picking the losers and finding the actual contenders.* We will explain this in the next two chapters.

Right now we are ready to take our final look into the crystal ball. This look is where we must compare the honest animals with each other and determine just how many, or how few of them we can throw out. This look is the over-all look—the total view—and it will show us something very important—namely, *whether the race is fit to play.*

The honest horses that we are now going to eliminate are animals which are getting a bet from the inside and who consequently will be in there fighting for the top hole, but who figure to miss nevertheless, because they are not good enough for this particular spot, which is, for them, a tough spot. And a tough spot for a race horse, experience will show, is usually a *losing spot.*

At this point, the Tote Board can no longer help us in picking losers. We must go beyond all convenient stop-and-go signs and make a few decisions.

We must realize that while the inside betting activity of the stable professionals is one of the most significant clues we can discover as to the approximate outcome of a given horse race—this action itself is often ill-advised (and sometimes downright mistaken), or, like the "best laid plans of mice and men" is very often wrong.

In short, the Third Man must read the past performances just the same as you do to calculate the chances of his horse today. He knows things about the animal that you don't know, of course, but then he reveals his intentions on the Tote Board. So that when we detect an inside bet, we know that we are dealing with "informed" speculation, at least. And this is always very valuable, although it is very far short of wisdom.

Trainers, by and large, are not particularly good handicappers. A lot of them, like a certain segment of the general public, depend on the opinions of the public handicappers. Where a trainer had the edge is—not in his ability to handicap a race—but in having intimate, up-to-date knowledge about his horse. But even this is mainly valuable for seeing when a horse has *no chance whatever*, perhaps because he's sick or sore.

So, while we can respect the conclusions of the Third Man in a negative sense—we can believe he *can't* win when he himself is of that opinion and doesn't even try—we cannot always respect his positive aspirations, that is, his idea that he *can* win in a particular spot, where it may actually seem that his horse has some chance.

A trainer's hopes are colored by many things. When he's trying, he almost always over-estimates his chance, because he *wants* to win. And the wish becomes father to the thought. When he loses after "sending" a horse he curses fate and talks about bad racing luck.

However, while there may be a thousand things that can happen to beat a well-meant horse, from the time he leaves the starting gate till he crosses the finish wire, bad racing luck in itself cannot be held responsible for too much of the animal's trouble.

What sends him down to defeat is one or more of the following factors that we have been considering all along, while eliminating sure-fire losers:

A well-meant animal will generally lose, despite all inside bets and good intentions, if the trainer makes the mistakes of sending him when:

> *He will be off-form.*
> *The company will be too rough.*
> *The pace will be too hot.*
> *The distance will be wrong.*
> *He will not be favored by the track or track condition.*

When we can determine that a well-meant horse will be at a disadvantage on *any combination* of these counts, and particularly in the department of *Class*, it may be that we can eliminate such an animal from our calculations on a given race, along with the sure-fire losers.

This is especially true if at the same time the animal finds himself "up against it" in the general pattern of the competition. For, remember, in horse racing everything is relative and every race is different.

Here, then, are ten minus-sign flags to guide you in finding the losing spot for certain well-meant animals:

1. *The Track Handicapper's Conditions Definitely Favor Another Horse or Horses.*

The Condition Book at a track is framed in advance of the meeting and is designed to spread purse money around. However, when the conditions say, "non-winners of a race" since such and such a date, or "non-winners of two races," or "non-winners of $3,000," etc., the Book *favors* horses who have run second or just missed a number of times, or horses who have not been racing at all, or horses that have won, say, $2,999. And this is just one example. These "conditions" should be studied carefully for angles on the race in other directions. Not only "form" angles, but "class" and "distance" angles as well will occur to you as you read the stipulations for eligibility in a given race.

2. *The Animal Has Not Been Racing Recently.*

It is a recognized fact that most winners of horse races have been raced within a week of their front-end effort. Likewise, another high percentage of winners comes from the category of animals which have been raced within the past two weeks. This is particularly true of the cheaper types of horses, since as we explained previously these animals can be brought into condition *only* by racing them. This does not mean, however, that a horse cannot win after a long lay-off. It certainly happens—but the horse does it usually because he has been freshened by the lay-off, and wins *despite* the lack of racing. Workouts must always be watched carefully for this sort of thing.

3. *The Hot Jockeys Are on Other Horses.*

There are definitely such things as "hot" and "cold" jockeys. Like horses, jockeys get out of shape for one reason or another and fall out of favor with trainers. Consequently, they do not get to ride the "live" horses. A trainer is superstitious about jockeys, also, and when he is shooting for the marbles he may even try to get the boy who won with the animal last time it won. When you find a "stiff" jockey aboard a well-meant horse, it may mean only that the trainer could get no other boy. Consult the box-score on jockeys for the current meet (in the program or in the *Daily Racing Form*) to see which boys are currently showing good riding form.

4. *The Animal Does Not Win Many Races or Much Money.*

Obviously, a horse that wins a lot of races (one out of four is pretty good) or a lot of money on a few races, is a good animal, and is to be preferred to his inferiors in this matter. However, to be fair to the horse, we must always ask, "What is his *percentage* of winnings—and in what *class bracket?*"

5. *The Horse Is Too Old, or Too Young, Relative to the Others.*

An old man cannot usually compete well with a young man, physically speaking. But then a very young man cannot usually compete well with a man in his prime. On this matter use horse sense.

6. *The Animal Is Carrying Too Much Weight.*

There is no question whatever that weight will slow down a race horse—but sometimes there is far too much noise made about five or ten pounds more or less on the back of an animal himself weighing 1,000 pounds. The farther the distance, of course, the heavier ten pounds will get. Also, horses differ in their physical stamina. Some animals carry weight better than others. Check the past performances and see how a horse performs under different weight assignments.

7. *The Animal Is a Filly or Mare Racing Against Geldings or Males.*

The female of the species is usually weaker (not slower) than the male, but there are exceptions to all rules. Mainly, they have less stamina, and at a route distance they probably are at a certain disadvantage. During the summer mating phase they may not perform well at all.

8. *The Animal Has a Poor Post Position for His Style of Running.*

Slow-breaking horses will generally do better from a middle or outside post position, while fast-breaking animals are definitely favored the closer to the rail they can get. A horse that can go to the front at once can save a world of ground by hugging the rail, if he doesn't have to knock himself out getting over there. A slow-breaker mainly needs to keep out of trouble (interference) during the early stages of the race, so that he can keep within striking distance of the leaders. Any horse who will be forced to run wide, and go the "overland" (outside) route will simply have to run farther than the others, and this can certainly beat him.

9. *The Animal Is Erratic or Highly Inconsistent.*

These animals usually have some physical trouble—in the legs or the breathing—and they are not to be trusted. However, they are hard to eliminate when they have talent, because who knows when they will show it? The only possible rule here is to favor a steady horse against these animals, other things being equal.

10. *The Animal Is a Faint-hearted Type.*

Such horses are to be despised even when they win, which is not too often. There is nothing worse than a quitter, and when we can determine that a horse has this tendency to give up when challenged, we should give him a big black mark. These true quitters (but be sure you're dealing with the true article) have broken more bankrolls than any other type of animal on the turf.

Any one of the above burdens can seriously diminish an honest horse's chances of getting down on the front end. In fact, if you can pin a couple of these minus signs on the animal, you may be able to throw him out of the race with no further ado. We are not interested in whether he is good enough to run second or third, but only in whether he is good enough to *win!*

And we must emphasize again that, while we are certainly interested in throwing out of a race horses who do not figure to be actual contenders, *we are by no means concerned with the idea of throwing out all but one horse.*

As a matter of fact, as we will explain later, the race that's fit to play is hardly ever the race where there is only one standout horse. A race with only one standout animal is just as bad, for our strategy, as a race in which most of the animals are actual contenders.

So, we must never, under any circumstances, gamble on throwing out of a race a horse who has a good chance to win that race. It doesn't matter if we come up with eight contenders in a nine-horse race. We must not throw out a beetle that *figures*. When we run into a race in which most of the animals are actual contenders, we simply don't play!

Generally speaking, *the race fit to play is that race where there is neither too few, nor too many actual contenders relative to the number of horses in the race and relative to the odds-spread that we read on the Tote Board.*

11. A RACE THAT'S FIT TO PLAY

THERE IS AN OLD proverb which says, "If you dance every set, you'll knock yourself out."

Everybody who plays the horses ought to have this great piece of wisdom engraved on his brain—because any man that plays every race on a given day or at a given meet is a mortal cinch to go bust. For, *many races are not fit to play!*

And yet, the public, has a tendency to do just this. Joe Blow can't bear to stand around. He wants action. Any kind of action, just so long as it's action. He looks at a race and at the Tote Board, and he sees clearly that he's up against it, but nevertheless he rushes up to the window and makes a bet. He *must* have something riding.

There's nothing wrong about playing the races for kicks, or thrills, or to while away the afternoon when you have nothing better to do, except that it's the most expensive form of recreation known to man. Even a two-dollar bettor can lose quite a bundle, over a period of time, when he plays the horses in this manner. If he bets more than two dollars, and has a gambling streak in his nature, he can lose a fortune.

A moment's thought should convince Joe that a race track is a business enterprise and that the management and stockholders expect a good return on their investment. With a 15% bite taken out of every dollar that passes through the parimutuel machines, it should be crystal clear that if the *same* dollar gets clipped seven times, there is nothing left.

Fortunately, the same dollar does not get clipped seven times because there is always fresh money coming into play, out of the public pocket. However, the actual *take*—track cut and taxes—that comes out of the money the collective public brings to a race track adds up to a king-sized bite.

When the short-priced horses win, this bite gets even bigger, because the public then *plays back* this *same* money, over and over. This is the deep-down reason why a track likes to see the low-priced horses win—and a good track handicapper will try to shape up his races to achieve this result, while sprinkling a few long-shots here and there, to "keep 'em coming." When too many longshots win, the track suffers from a diminished play-back.

How does the track handicapper do this? He can't control the way a race will turn out. He can't foretell *the* winner any better than you, or Joe Blow, or the trainer. But he can more or less control the *type* of race it will turn out to be—that is, a short-priced mutuel or an upset mutuel type of race.

He does this by the way he sets up his conditions of eligibility and by his assignments of weight. He does it by allowing into a race many animals who will be *actual contenders*. In short, he does it by creating races in which the winner may by any one of a half-dozen horses all at more or less short prices. *In fact, he does it by creating almost every day a certain number of races that are not fit to play!*

These races are beautifully fit to play from the viewpoint of the track, because they result in more profit to the track, as explained above. But from the viewpoint of a smart horseplayer, such races are to be avoided like the plague.

There are certain types of races the track handicapper

offers you almost every day that you should toss back to him by refusing to play! Many of these races will be those in which we have no past record of the horses to study, because there is no past record. We mean a race with all or many first-starters in it, whether this be a two-year-old race or a three-year-old race. Betting on a race of this type is like coming up to bat in a ball game with a blindfold on your head. It's hard enough to hit the ball with your eyes wide open.

Even a race with *one* first starter in it is a dangerous race to play. For, how do you know what sort of beast you are dealing with. To bet on him may be to throw money away. To eliminate him is foolish because he might very well be *the* winner. Even the Tote Board is a poor guide on first starters, since we have no notion of what the horse *should* be in line.

A smart horse-player will play only those races in which he has a past performance record on all of the horses. And each horse should have at least four or five races that we can study. This is essential.

Some experts advise players not to touch two-year-old races, jumping races, or races on off tracks, or very cheap claiming races, etc. But in our strategy this makes no difference whatever. In fact we welcome all such races, if the above requirement is met.

Other types of races not fit to play might be outlined roughly as follows, but these figures should not be taken as rigid rules, for there are always exceptions:

1. *A six-horse (or fewer) race with more than two actual contenders*

2. *A nine-horse (or fewer) race with more than three actual contenders*

3. *A twelve-horse (or fewer) race with more than four actual contenders.*

We want to emphasize that the above must not be taken as hard-and-fast rules, because what ultimately determines whether a race is fit to play is the closing Tote Board prices on the actual contenders.

In other words, there are races which may meet these specifications and yet still be races not fit to play. Just as there are certain races which may not exactly meet these specifications which will be beautifully fit to play. The odds-spread on the actual contenders gives us the stop or go sign, finally, in deciding to play a race or to pass it.

There is such a thing as a race having too few actual contenders to make it a race fit to play! When you have only one or two standout horses in a race (two actual contenders) the odds on the horse, or horses, may be so meager that the whole thing may not constitute a good wager, even if you win. You might bet a bundle, you say, and clean up, even though the odds are short. Well, you *might*—but then you might not! Horse racing being what it is, you should always ask for a fair shake for your money. And it's never a fair shake in a horse race, in our opinion, to be satisfied with very short prices, whether you're betting a buck or a million.

Remember, it's not the amount of money you win on any given race that keeps you on top, but the percentage of return on your speculation, over a period of time!

12. HOW TO BET THE WINNERS

MORE LONGSHOTS CAN be brought down, more winning tickets cashed, and more money made on the races by picking the losers and betting the actual contenders—then by trying to pick *the* winner and betting on this horse alone.

Now let's try to explain this fact. And once we do, we are at the end of the line—and the crystal ball is yours. As for how to bet your money, and in what amounts, there will be no question. It should be perfectly clear!

But, first, we must explode two myths which somehow have come down through the years, in the folklore of horse-playing, and which many horse-players have never even questioned. These old-wives' tales belong in the same category as the ones that say you can't eat fish and drink milk together, without getting sick.

Ask Joe Blow how you should bet your money at the race track, and he'll probably tell you:

1. Never bet more than one horse to win in the same race, because if you do, you'll be betting against yourself.

2. Always back up the horse you bet to Win with a Place bet, and maybe even a Show bet, too, because the horse might just miss, and you can still win a little or maybe just lose a little, instead of everything, if the animal gets second or third.

These two notions are so widespread among horse-players that it has never occurred to most of them that such an approach might be dead wrong, on both counts, and the principal reason, on the wagering side, why the average horse-player loses so much money at the races! That is, aside from the track take.

The smart way to bet horses is just the opposite, as indeed the smart way to pick horses is just the opposite.

How could it be otherwise? Since parimutuel horse-playing is a battle of wits between you and the public, you can't beat them by joining them in their mistakes, but only by taking advantage of their mistakes, *by reverse action!*

The smart way to bet the horses is:

1. Always bet more than one horse to Win in the same race, if the race is fit to play.

2. Never make a Place bet or a Show bet or a Combination bet at any time.

A horse race is a horse race, and while there is such a thing as a sure-fire loser, there is no such thing as a sure-fire winner, or even a sure-fire "in-the-money" horse. It is only after the race that the Monday-morning quarterbacks can see how such and such an animal "stood out." But before the race, they all "stood out."

Remember also that when you have a number of possible contenders in a race, the public betting will be confused, thus causing the Win odds on one or more of the actual contenders to rise.

It is precisely at this point, and in this kind of a race, that the smart horse-player can bet *all* of the actual contenders to win, and show a profit whichever one gets there—and sometimes a big profit, when a longshot contender comes down on top!

Experience with every imaginable "betting system" has proved that if you cannot beat the races by making *flat Win bets*, then you cannot beat them at all. In other words, you must cash a sufficient number of winning "on-the-nose" tickets, at odds high enough to compensate for all losing tickets, while still retaining a profit.

If it is impossible to do this consistently by picking and betting to Win one horse (*the* winner) in a race, how fantastic, then, to think it can be done by betting horses to Place or Show—where the mutuel pay-offs are notoriously shorter. To see just how much shorter they are, total up the pay-off prices on the winner of each race, for just one week— and look hard at the figures.

Whatever your betting unit happens to be, you risk one of these units every time you play a horse for *any* position. Therefore, to use one of these units carelessly (from some so-called safety-hedge motive) and to put it where it cannot possibly earn enough money to *overcompensate* your losses, *even when you collect*, is the surest way to become a chronic loser.

The public, it seems, does everything backwards when it comes to horse-playing. Joe Blow goes in for a lot of Place or Show betting , and even Combination (across the board) betting. He bets longshots to Place or to Show, and favorites to Win, when it should be as clear as the nose on his face that just the opposite should be done, if he must bet horses to Place or Show. For the Place and Show prices on long-shots are almost always pitiful, in comparison to the Win, while these same Place and Show prices *on favorites* are actually very good, by percentage comparison to the Win.

It must be emphasized also that there is no possible way of juggling the amounts of money you bet, or any conceivable combination of position plays, that can turn out half so well as making a flat bet to win on a race. There are hundreds of "systems" for betting the horses but they all add up to naught, because at bottom you must be able to show a profit on a flat Win bet, before the systems could be of any use to you.

So that the problem of winning on the races, *in a consistent sense* boils down to this contradiction:

1. Playing one horse to Win in a race, on a flat-bet basis, is the most successful method of wagering, superior to all forms of Place or Show betting, and to all forms of combination betting.

2. However, picking *the* winner of a horse race consistently is one of the hardest things in the world to do, and is the most unsuccessful approach to the problem of selecting horses, inferior to all forms of multiple selection, and to all forms of "in-the-money" selection.

How, then, can this contradiction be resolved? Certainly not by betting several horses in the same race to Place or to Show, or both. Nothing could break your bankroll faster. For no matter how many of them you got in, you could never *overcompensate* for your losers.

There is only *one* way—*multiple Win betting in the same race, on a flat-bet basis. That is, multiple Win betting of the actual contenders, in a race that's fit to play!*

This approach combines the best wagering method with the best selection approach, at the minimum expense of wagering units!

How many more winners do you think you can pick if you have, say, three horses running for you in a given race instead of one (who might get into trouble)? And how many more longshots do you think you can bring down (the uncertainty of *the* winner being what it is)?

You're right! Plenty more!

As for the objection that you may be betting against yourself—how can this be, if you play only those races in which you can show a profit *whichever* one of your horses wins? A profit, small or large, depending on which way the ball bounces!

If a race is fit to play, it will permit you to bet two, three, or even four horses to Win (depending on the number of horses in the race and the odds spread)—if you feel that all such horses are actual contenders. Naturally, one would never bet three horses in a race if he felt that only two horses in the race were actual contenders.

When you get an odds-spread of 5/2, 4/1 and 10/1, for instance, in a ten-horse race, say, it would be folly not to play them all, if you think they represent the actual contention in the race. For, if you bet any single one of them, and ignore the other two, you most certainly are betting against yourself. By expending only two additional units, you not only buy an insurance policy well worth the premium, but you get a triple free ride on beating the race—sometimes with a box-car mutuel!

We can now make a final definition of a race that's fit to play:

A race that's fit to play is any race wherein we can make a flat bet to Win on all of the actual contenders—and show a profit whichever one of them gets the decision at the wire.

If only one horse should represent all of the actual contention in a given race, as you see it, without emotional blinkers, then naturally this one horse becomes a play—if you can get a reasonable price on the animal. These races are pretty rare, and on the whole nothing much will be lost by passing them up entirely. You must run without insurance, remember, and bad racing luck can stop any animal.

Here are a few suggested rules-of-thumb: (you can bend them a little):

IN A SIX-HORSE (OR FEWER) RACE, if you see only *two* actual contenders, and you can get at least Even Money on one of them and *more* on the other, you have a play—if you care to make it.

IN A NINE-HORSE (OR FEWER) RACE, if you see only *three* actual contenders, and you can get at least 2-1 on one of them and more on the other two, you have a play—if you care to make it.

IN A TWELVE-HORSE (OR FEWER) RACE, if you see only *four* actual contenders, and you can get at least 3-1 on one of them and more on the other three, you have a play—if you care to make it.

It is difficult to place a bet at exactly the odds shown on the Tote Board at closing time, since the odds will change somewhat after you make your bet, no matter how late you try to make it. This is important, however, on your lowest-priced horse only, since it is not likely that very late changes will make the race unplayable on your other horse, or horses. If a horse closes at Even, or 2-1 or 3-1, he will always pay more than Even, 2-1 or 3-1, so that you realize a very small profit on the race, if this particular animal turns out to be *the* winner.

Obviously it is one of the *other* animals you hope to bring down, and *will bring down* a surprising number of times at surprising mutuel pay-offs!

Now, a race may be fit to play, *and you may not care to play it*. For, it still may not present a very attractive wagering proposition. This can happen when the actual contenders, while meeting the specifications, do not present an odds-spread that is sufficiently attractive.

The odds-spread on the actual contenders is not only what determines whether a race is fit to play, *but whether it is worth-while to play! Some races are not worth-while to play even if you should win a small amount of money on them.* As we said before, a player should always ask for a fair shake on his speculation. So, why feel compelled to jump in and play any given race, when races are being run every day and when better spots will turn up by waiting?

Here are a few examples of attractive and unattractive races fit to play:

Attractive	Even and 3-1 or more
Unattractive	Even and 2-1 or less
Attractive	2-1 and 4-1 and 6-1 or more
Unattractive	2-1 and 3-1 and 4-1 or less
Attractive	3-1 and 7-1 and 10-1 and 15-1 or more
Unattractive	3-1 and 5-1 and 6-1 and 8-1 or less

The most attractive types of all, of course, and if you can wait, you will find them, are:

> Even and 5-1 or more
> 2-1 and 6-1 and 15-1 or more
> 3-1 and 8-1 and 15-1 and 20-1 or more
> 3-1 and 10-1 and 30-1 and 40-1 or more

Never think that these latter figures are exaggerated. Remember that the Third Man is always gunning for such prices, and that most of the amazing pay-offs at a race track are on *horses that were not only "sent" but bet on by the stable.* When you play all of the actual contenders in a race you get these kinds of prices—prices you can rarely get playing only one horse in a race.

And with good mutuel pay-offs you will be in a position to *overcompensate* those races that will invariably let you down once in a while. You will be able to make up for those losses and stay ahead of the game—*if you do the selection job carefully, and the betting job as coldly as you can!*

13. "PURE" HANDICAPPING

"PURE" HANDICAPPING is the *first* thing a player must get acquainted with if he wants to beat the game. By "pure" handicapping we mean the question of whether or not a horse has a chance, in a given race, apart from the fact that somebody may or may not be betting on him. Pure handicapping deals with the basic factors of Form, Class, Time, Distance and Footing, and cares nothing at all about the Tote Board. If there were no betting on horse races, and trainers therefore had no motive for manipulating their animals, then pure handicapping would be all that a player would need to know. He could pick the losers and spot the actual contenders almost every time.

Even as it stands, with all the monkey-business that goes on around a race track, pure handicapping is still absolutely indispensable *for picking losers*. For a good pure handicapper can very often tell you that a certain horse is a loser, despite the fact the stable is betting its shirt on the animal. In other words, *in certain cases, the pure handicapper knows more than the stable itself.*

This kind of knowledge means dollars and cents saved in your pocket, if nothing more. If most horse-players knew just enough about handicapping to lay off certain horses, they would save a bundle every year, even if they never had a winner!

In almost every race there are horses entered that can be picked as losers—*even apart from the odds board!* This is the great *negative* advantage a good pure handicapper has over the general public.

On the *positive* side, unfortunately, pure handicapping runs into trouble. While it can pick the *possible* contenders, in a given horse race, it is at a loss to pick the *actual* contenders. This is because it has no way of knowing whether or not a trainer is going to "send" an animal that can very well win if it tries.

This is a serious deficiency, and the primary reason why so many good handicappers do not seem to be able to win money at the races. They hardly ever bet "impossible" animals and very frequently they come up with live contenders —but, somehow, something seems to "work against them." You can hear them swear at times at a jockey, and insist that the horse they bet would have won but for the stupidity of the midget on his back. Or, they will howl about bad racing luck—a horse getting into a jam, or going wide into the stretch, or getting "left" at the start.

All of these things happen, of course, *but sometimes they happen on purpose!*

Nevertheless, the pure handicapper is in a position to beat the races, because he knows the fundamentals of the game. He is a graduate of grade school, at least, whereas most of the public is still in kindergarten. What troubles he has can be corrected by a short course in "smart-money" handicapping (See Chapter 14).

Most horse-players need to spend more time studying past performance charts. For every hour spent pouring over these charts (at leisure, not at the track before the race), they would find the pay big, *in terms of money saved, if not yet in money won.*

The Chart Studies which follow in this chapter are designed to show you the sort of thing to look for when you study actual racing charts. *They deal with the fundamentals of pure handicapping, not the fine points.* As a horse-player becomes skilled in reading charts, and gives himself the opportunity to watch the actual running of the races he studies, his ability to spot losers and contenders will grow by leaps and bounds. Dozens of fine points will occur to him and become part of his equipment for outsmarting the crowd.

There is no substitute for pure handicapping. It is the foundation upon which all "smart-money" handicapping is built. And there is absolutely no substitute for being your own handicapper. For in a game which is strictly a battle of wits between you and the mass of horse-players, *how* else can you get the jump on the public, which takes, or buys, selections available to everybody? In this business, as in any other, there is no short-cut to success.

CHART STUDY A: *Coming Into Form*

Horses do not usually "burst" into form but are raced into their best condition after they have been dull for a time, or when they come back into racing after a layoff of some months. Either sudden *early speed, stout late speed,* or *speed in spots* is the tip-off they are moving up on the form cycle and that further improvement can be expected.

Here are a few abbreviated charts designed to show the general "pattern" you should be on the lookout for:

DATE	DISTANCE	1ST CALL	2ND CALL	STRETCH	FINISH	TIME OF RACE
Jly 31	6f	*1–1*	*1–1*	*1–1*	*1–1*	1:11
Jly 15	6f	*1–1*	*2–2*	*2–4*	*5–6*	1:11
Jly 1	6f	*2–2*	*2–1*	*6–8*	*10–10*	1:11

Reading from the bottom up, we see that beginning on July 1 the animal showed the *early speed* signal, came back on July 15 with more early speed, plus greater staying power, and finally on July 31 moved into a nice win. We have kept the distance of six furlongs and the time of 1:11 (one minute and eleven seconds) the same in order to illustrate the point. Actual charts will never appear this simple, nor an animal's progress quite so straightforward—because there will be changes of distance, class and track condition, and even tracks, to discount. However, the idea is to grasp this pattern, because it is perhaps the most fundamental thing in all pure handicapping. When an animal is on the upgrade, in this fashion, he can get so good from one race to the next you will hardly believe your eyes.

Remember that in horse racing everything is moving, nothing stands still. *A horse is getting better or he is getting worse*—he never stays the same. If you pick him today on what he did last week, without trying to determine whether he is on the way up, or on the way down, you will be disappointed time and again.

Sometimes a horse will show the same kind of improvement, *but in the opposite manner*—through *late speed*:

DATE	DISTANCE	1ST CALL	2ND CALL	STRETCH	FINISH	TIME OF RACE
Jly 31	6f	6–5	5–4	4–2	1–1	1:11
Jly 15	6f	7–7	6–6	5–6	4–2	1:11
Jly 1	6f	10–10	10–10	10–8	5–3	1:11

Here, you will note, the form sign came on July 1, with the animal closing fast to gain five lengths in the stretch, after being outrun for the greater part of the race. When a horse has been running "dead" and then suddenly shows this sign, you can rest assured he is improving.

Very often the form sign comes, not in early speed or in late speed but in *speed in spots*. Somewhere along the way, in the running of the race, the animal makes a bold move, only to flatten out or stop rather suddenly, and perhaps finish last in the race.

DATE	DISTANCE	1ST CALL	2ND CALL	STRETCH	FINISH	TIME OF RACE
Jly 31	6f	*1–1*	*1–1*	*1–2*	*1–3*	1:11
Jly 15	6f	*8–8*	*2–hd*	*5–4*	*8–8*	1:11
Jly 1	6f	*12–15*	*8–7*	*1–1*	*12–20*	1:11

Here, the form sign came on July 1 when the horse actually moved up and took the lead in the stretch, only to stop dead in his tracks "like he was hit in the head." Stopping or no stopping, when you see this sort of thing, it is a powerful sign—and never let 20 beaten lengths scare you off. When an animal is on the upgrade, he will astound you by how he can go on—after stopping in his previous races.

Actually, there is only a small number of real "stoppers" among horses. When an animal is beaten 20 lengths, after he has been up there, it is usually because he is just coming into form—or more usually, because he is being eased up by the jockey.

Horses usually go out of form more suddenly than they come into it. Sometimes it is because of a physical ailment, or bad legs, or breathing trouble. It is easy to see on the chart. Where formerly they were peppy, they now seem "dead." However, many horses do get stale, and then they decline in power in just about the opposite manner of that shown on the charts for improvement. *Always make sure you see the "pattern of improvement" (as indicated by several races), rather than the "pattern of decline."*

CHART STUDY B: *Step-Up and Step-Down*

Horses are usually stepped up as they improve their condition (get hotter), and stepped down as they begin to tail off (go stale). This is the natural course of things.

The reason is obvious. If a trainer is going to win races with a horse, he must always try to find the spot to suit the animal's *present* ability. He must run the beast where it has a chance, if it is tailing off. If it is getting better, he must step it up to keep from losing it for a song, by the claim process, to some other trainer.

However, all this calls for good judgment, and not all trainers have this kind of horse sense. Some run an animal in claiming races for $6,000 when the beetle should be running for $3,000, or less, if it ever hopes to win.

But top-notch trainers are pretty shrewd, on the whole, and have a sixth sense about just where to put a horse at a given point in his form cycle. A horse-player has to use good judgment, too. He has to disagree very often with the *average sort of trainer.* He has to decide whether this fellow really knows what he is doing.

For there is nothing that will beat an animal more surely than running him with company that is too tough. No matter how fast the time of the beast with cheaper ones, he is riding for a fall every time he is stepped up.

With smart trainers, horses that begin to show form signs at *high* class brackets are often *stepped down* for the win:

DATE	DISTANCE	1ST CALL	2ND CALL	STRETCH	FINISH	CLASS OF RACE
Aug 17	6f	1–1	1–2	1–2	1–1	2500
Aug 7	6f	1–1	2–2	4–5	4–8	4500
Aug 4	6f	1–1	4–5	5–7	8–9	6000

Note that the form sign came with early speed on August 4, at a bracket of $6,000. More signs came, with better staying power, on August 7, with a drop-down to $4,500. The trainer knew then the beast was ready to fly for the target, on August 17, with another drop-down.

When you see this kind of pattern—gradual form improvement and gradual drop-down—you are dealing with a very dangerous horse and a trainer who knows his business. Such trainers, who know just *how much to* drop a horse, and *when,* win many races with their animals, and are to be reckoned with at all times.

Other trainers, not so shrewd, will do *this* sort of thing with such an animal:

DATE	DISTANCE	1ST CALL	2ND CALL	STRETCH	FINISH	CLASS OF RACE
Aug 17	6f	4–4	6–6	7–8	8–10	*6000*
Aug 7	6f	*1–1*	*2–2*	*4–5*	4–8	*4500*
Aug 4	6f	*1–1*	*4–5*	*5–7*	8–9	*6000*

Here, everything is the same except for the August 17 race, where, instead of dropping the animal, this trainer steps him up to $6,000, and gets him beaten soundly. This type of trainer, when he has an improving beast on his hands, gets excited and thinks he can beat the world. He also dreams of a fat mutuel price, on account of the step-up.

Some animals, *when they are on the downgrade,* will not be helped by a step-down, not even a sharp drop. We must not be misled by these animals *when we sense a pattern of decline.* Note the following: (*Read from bottom up.*)

DATE	DISTANCE	1ST CALL	2ND CALL	STRETCH	FINISH	CLASS OF RACE
Feb. 1	6f	8–8	7–8	8–8	12–10	*2000*
Jan. 1	6f	10–10	10–12	12–20	12–20	*4000*
Dec. 1	6f	7–8	8–8	*10–10*	10–20	*7500*
Nov. 1	6f	6–8	5–5	8–9	10–10	*10000*
Oct. 1	6f	4–2	3–2	*2–1*	4–5	*15000*

The important thing to grasp here is the *pattern,* and incidentally the infrequent racing dates—a month apart—indicating trouble. Horses that are okay are usually sent to the races more often than this during a given racing season.

Needless to say, the general public drops thousands and thousands of dollars on this type of horse, because they think each time he "steps down" he will be a sure winner. Whereas, the trainer is hoping, each time, some other gullible trainer will claim the animal.

We must always ask the question, on either a step-up or a step-down—*"is the trainer trying to win, or is he trying to do something else?"* Often, a step-up is for conditioning purposes (give the beast a tough race) and very often a drop-down is a desperation move (the animal is going sour).

When an animal is stepped up in a serious attempt to win at the higher bracket, it is usually because he is showing very obvious hot form at low brackets, perhaps winning. It is not too hard to distinguish this type of beast from the one being stepped up for heavy exercise only. In the latter case there is something wild, almost fantastic, about the step-up. We know the horse doesn't belong in such company. In the former case, it seems more like a logical improvement.

Here is the step-up for conditioning purposes:

DATE	DISTANCE	1ST CALL	2ND CALL	STRETCH	FINISH	CLASS OF RACE
Oct. 1	6f	*1–1*	5–6	10–15	12–20	*10000*
Sep. 9	6f	2–3	3–4	*4–5*	6–6	4000
Sep. 1	6f	8–4	7–4	6–5	9–7	2500

The trainer, here, has an improving animal on his hands that may be able to win at around $5,000 pretty soon. Right now, he is getting the beast ready.

Here is the step-up and serious try to win:

DATE	DISTANCE	1ST CALL	2ND CALL	STRETCH	FINISH	CLASS OF RACE
Oct. 1	6f	*1–1*	*1–hd*	4–3	4–4	*10000*
Sep. 9	6f	1–1	1–1	1–2	1–4	6000
Sep. 1	6f	1–2	1–2	1–2	1–2	4000

This was a legitimate try (October 1) and the horse simply was not good enough for $10,000 class. He might drop down o about $7,500 and win in that class.

When all this is remembered, we must nevertheless be on guard against making a too-hasty decision that a horse is overmatched when he loses the first time, after a step-up. Sometimes, an abnormal condition—such as an off track or a wrong distance—or bad racing luck, and not the step-up, sends him down to defeat. If this is the case, he very often comes right back at the same high bracket and wins:

Here is an obvious case of bad racing luck, on June 30, with the proof coming with the stout win on July 4:

DATE	DISTANCE	1ST CALL	2ND CALL	STRETCH	FINISH	CLASS OF RACE
Jly 4	6f	1–1	1–1	1–2	1–3	5000
Jun 30	6f	12–15	12–12	12–20	12–20	5000
Jun 22	6f	1–1	1–1	1–1	1–2	3000
Jun 15	6f	1–2	1–3	1–2	1–1	2500

You must almost always throw out such a race, as the June 30 type, in the record of an animal which is showing good stuff otherwise. Obviously, something happened to the beast and the effort does not represent his true ability.

Another instance of something wrong:

DATE	DISTANCE	1ST CALL	2ND CALL	STRETCH	FINISH	CLASS OF RACE
June 1	6f	4–2	3–1	2–1	1–1	6000
May 20	1 1/16	1–3	1–5	4–3	10–10	6000
May 15	7f	1–2	1–1	1–hd	1–ns	4000
May 10	6f	1–1	1–2	1–3	1–2	3000

This animal, basically a sprinter, and in the hottest kind of form—had to struggle to win the May 15 race at seven furlongs, a distance already a trifle too far for his best performance. The trainer then (perhaps to get a price) overestimated the animal's ability and sent him forth at one mile and one-sixteenth, on May 20, and at the same time stepped him up to $6,000. When he sent the horse back at six furlongs (dropping distance), at the same class brackets of $6,000, on June 1, he won again.

Some horses are erratic about running on wet tracks. One time they will run in the mud (or on slow or sloppy footing) and the next time they won't. So, when such a beast is stepped up (because he is in hot form), and then catches a sloppy track, the trainer is holding his breath. Very often he lets it out with a string of cuss words (*on February 16*):

DATE	TRACK CONDITION	1ST CALL	2ND CALL	STRETCH	FINISH	CLASS OF RACE
Mar 2	fast	*1–1*	*1–1*	*1–1*	*1–2*	*4500*
Feb. 16	*sloppy*	8–7	8–9	6–6	7–8	*4500*
Feb. 8	fast	*1–1*	*1–1*	*1–3*	*1–1*	*3500*
Feb. 1	slow	1–1	1–1	1–2	1–2	*2000*

This animal's failure, on February 16, was quite obviously due to the "off" track, as his snappy come-back on a fast track on March 2 proves.

These same things can happen when an animal is stepped down to win. On the first try, on the step-down, he catches an "off" track, or is run at a wrong distance, and blows the race. Next time, with suitable footing, or proper distance, he wins very handily.

These are the main form factors to check out on all step-ups or step-downs. *Never make a hasty decision.* Think it over!

CHART STUDY C: *Staying on the Pace*

The underlying reason why cheap horses can't beat classy horses—not even when the race has a slowish final time—is that *somewhere along the way the pace gets too hot.* The cheap animal is clobbered down, either early or late, and he winds up running a slower race than he usually runs when pitched with his own kind.

However, this business of not being able to keep up— usually in the early stages of a sprint, or the late stages of a route race—is not confined to cheap ones running against good ones. It also happens when cheap ones meet other cheap ones who happen to have *a better pace ability* for a certain distance. This is obvious when we see routers who can't keep up in a sprint race, and sprinters who can't stay on top in a route race.

But the problem is far more complex than this. There is such a thing as a horse being able to stay on the pace of a seven-furlong (7f) race, and not being able to stay on the pace of a six-furlong (6f) race. Being able to stay on the pace of a mile race, and not being able to stay on the pace of a seven-furlong race, etc. It is hard to convince many horse-players of this fact. They can't seem to dig the idea that a horse which figures strongly at six furlongs does not necessarily figure at seven furlongs. Or, one that figures strongly at seven furlongs does not necessarily figure at six furlongs.

Why do so many players find this hard to believe, and continue to throw their money away betting horses which are going the "wrong distance"? It may be because they have never really sat down and analyzed the pace times of races at different distances.

Here is a tabulation showing the fractional (pace) times for four different races at four different distances—all run on the same day, at the same track, and all at approximately the same class:

	1/4 MILE	1/2 MILE	3/4 MILE	7/8 MILE	1 MILE	1 1/16
SIX FURLONGS	22 3/5	46 1/5	1:11			
SEVEN FURLONGS	22 4/5	46 4/5	1:12	1:25		
1 MILE	23 1/5	47 2/5	1:13		1:39 1/5	
1 1/16 MILE	24 1/5	48 3/5	1:14 2/5		1.41 2/5	1:48 4/5

It is clear from this chart that the longer the race, the slower the fractional times become. If you will forget, for the moment, that some horses can do well at several different distances, you will see that ordinarily (that is, usually) a seven-furlong horse will not be able to keep up at six furlongs, a mile horse will not be able to keep up at seven furlongs, etc. It should also be clear that the animals in the two sprint races (6f and 7f) could not continue to run farther *at the same rate of speed.* They would not only slow down, they might even collapse. Hence, they would not be able to keep up with the two route-race animals in the late stages of longer races.

It is even more precise than this. Most true six-furlong horses will run out of gas before they get to the seven-furlong finish, and most true seven-furlong horses will falter before they get to the mile finish.

So it goes, and all trainers are very well aware of it. They know that each horse in the barn has a "best distance," a distance at which he is far more likely to win than at any other. Say a trainer had five horses in training, and he either had it written down, or in his mind, that their records were as follows:

BEST TIME EVER ACHIEVED AT DISTANCE

	SIX FURLONGS	SEVEN FURLONGS	ONE MILE	MILE AND SIXTEENTH
Big Beetle	1:11	*1:24*	1:40	1:48
Middle Kick	1:12	1:25	*1:38*	1:47
Slow Moe	1:14	1:28	1:42	1:50
Short 'n Sweet	*1:10*	1:26	1:41	1:49
Roy the Router	1:13	1:27	1:39	*1:46*

If these animals were all of the same class, and all in good condition, which one would you bet, if they raced against one another four times, at four different distances? The answer is obvious. *A different one each time!* The only horse which is no good at *any* distance is Slow Moe. This type of beetle is never worth a bet—in any spot!

While these tables have been simplified (they are *not* scientific representations), the point should nevertheless be clear that an animal's ability to stay on the pace, in a given horse race, is closely related to his "best time for the distance." *If an animal has a "slow" time for a given distance, having raced that distance a number of times, it is no doubt because he can't stay on the usual pace times for that distance.* (See CHART STUDY D for specific comment on "Best Time for Distance.")

Now that all this has been said, however, we must face the fact that the question of staying on the pace is more complicated yet. It is more complicated because several horses in the same race may each have excellent time for the distance. How are we going to separate them?

This is the best question in all pure handicapping!

Let's say we are trying to separate horses at six furlongs, where each animal has the same time of 1:10 flat for the distance. We have checked them out on condition, class, etc., and find them about equal. Which ones are going to be there or thereabouts at the finish—and which ones are not?

Let's look at the past performance charts of three such beetles:

	DISTANCE	1ST CALL	2ND CALL	STRETCH	FINISH	TIME OF RACE
No. 1	6f	1–1	1–1	1–1	1–1	*1:10*
No. 2	6f	5–5	5–4	4–3	1–hd	*1:10*
No. 3	6f	10–10	8–6	5–4	1–ns	*1:10*

If these three animals go in a race against one another, the chances are that No. 1 will win in a handy way, even though both No. 2 and No. 3 are capable of the same final time of 1:10.

We admit that this sounds like a mathematical absurdity, yet the fact remains it happens every day—and the players who go by "time" lose money taking a chance against No. 1, because the others have the "same time." To add insult to injury, No. 1 *often wins such a race in a final time of 1:11!* For some reason that remains a mystery to the hard-luck player, No. 2 or No. 3 doesn't even get in the money!

This is the sort of thing that causes some players to tear up their racing papers and say the form charts are "a lot of bunko," and "you're better off if you don't even look at them." Others, more violently, complain the whole racing game is "crooked" and that they were the victims of a "boat race" (rigged race).

The hard truth of the matter is, however, that animal No. 2 and animal No. 3 were *outrun—and they figured to fare badly in any race with a stiff early pace.* Slow-breaking horses always run the risk of getting "left" and losing practically all chance—at the outset of the race. A horse may have an excellent final time for a given race, but he cannot uncork that time if he is a sluggish beginner and catches a hot pace in the first quarter.

But even when the horse keeps on fighting, after getting behind 10 lengths or more at the quarter, he still has to work his way up through the field, where he might be blocked, or have to run wide, etc. All these things clip fractions and even seconds off his final time.

The moral of all this is that in horse racing there is always a great advantage to the animal that can run "all the way." Some horses have brilliant early speed and others have brilliant late speed—but the animals which win the most races are those that have "all-the-way" speed. However, in comparing horses in the past performance charts, do not hastily assume that an animal which has "all-the-way" speed against cheapsters will be able to show the same talent when he is stepped up. In the previous example, we were dealing with horses of the same class.

Let's look at the picture again, when the class ratings are different:

	DIS-TANCE	1ST CALL	2ND CALL	STRETCH	FINISH	TIME OF RACE	CLASS OF RACE	FINAL TIME OF HORSE
No. 1	6f	1–1	1–1	1–1	1–1	*1:10*	*3000*	1:10
No. 2	6f	5–5	5–4	4–3	5–5	*1:09*	*8000*	1:10
No. 3	6f	1–1	1–hd	3–3	4–5	*1:09*	*12000*	1:10

Here, the final time of the three horses is the same, since we allow $\frac{1}{5}$ of a second for each beaten length. But the whole picture is now changed, because of the class differential, and the manner in which the times were achieved!

Which of these three animals would be the likely winner if they were raced together? . . . and why? Well, let's start by eliminating animal No. 1, not just because he is cheap, but because he clearly won't be able to stay on the pace, much less show the front-running ability he did against his own kind. The pace in this race is going to be murderous—and No. 3 is going out to set it. We know this, because he was on top for about a half-mile in his previous race at $12,000—at pace times which had to be sensational, because of the final time of the race: 1:09.

Animal No. 2 cannot be eliminated, because he is capable

of drawing up neck and neck with No. 3, in the stretch, after being four or five lengths behind in the early stages. We know this because he too comes off a race with the hot final time of 1:09.

Will No. 2 catch No. 3 and be the winner?

The chances are very good that he will not!

We say this because it is very likely that an animal with the pace ability and staying power of No. 3 will run an even faster race against horses he can draw away from, at the half-mile pole.

Where will No. 1 finish? The chances are that No. 1 will be beaten by about 20 lengths, and show a final time of 1:13 or worse. Yet there is nothing wrong with No. 1. He is in hot form. He was simply overmatched. He can come back in a day or two at a lower class bracket and run away with the race, in a final time of 1:10!

This is why the number of lengths a horse wins by, or loses by, in one race is meaningless as a guide in predicting what he will do in another race, where the conditions of class, or distance, are changed.

Pace handicapping is the most difficult part of all pure handicapping. And yet, if we try to visualize how the pace will shape up in a race, it will become clear that certain animals *will*, and others *will not*, be able to keep up. *If they can't keep up, in the early stages, they can't win—nine times out of ten!*

Among those who can keep up, we must use the other factors, such as Form, Class, Distance, etc., to make the separation.

CHART STUDY D: *Best Time for Distance*

It cannot be emphasized too often that horses with a potential good time for a certain distance are always dangerous when they are going that specific distance. When other things are equal among the horses in a given race—such as condition, class, etc.—this factor of "best time for the distance" is your touchstone for handicapping the race.

At the top of the past performances for each race in your daily racing paper, there is a table showing the best recent time each horse in the race has achieved for the distance of today's race. It looks like this:

SIX AND ONE-HALF FURLONGS

HORSE	DATE	TRACK	RECORD	WEIGHT CARRIED
Cheap Jack	May 15	A	1:17	120
Cheap Jill	Jun 1	Y	1:19⅗	110
Sometimes Sue	Apr 6	X	1:17	115
Pan Flash	Jan 7	X	1:21	110
Throat Latcher	Mar 4	A	1:17⅗	103
Betting Tool	Sep 10	Y	1:16⅘	120

In analyzing this table, it is necessary to take into account the "fastness" or "slowness" of the different tracks and make the necessary adjustments. Also, we must allow for the amount of weight carried when the good or bad time was made, as against the amount of weight being carried today (this latter fact appears right next to the horse's name in the entries).

Let's say that Track A is the "fastest" track and the track record there for this distance is 1:14. Track X is "average", with track record of 1:15. Track Y is "slowest" with track record of 1:16. We get this information by consulting the "Comparative Track Record Table" which is published by racing papers periodically, and kept up to date.

After mulling over this situation for a while, we see that our information indicates that Betting Tool has absolutely the best time for this distance of 6½ furlongs, and that therefore he might be dangerous today, especially if he has been showing form signs (perhaps at some other distance) and is not outclassed today.

The table also indicates that Cheap Jill may not have much chance today, with Betting Tool in there, since her time is three full seconds slower, on records from the same Track Y. We might decide to eliminate her from our calculations on the race.

Sometimes Sue has a best time of 1:17 at Track X, an "average" speed track, where the track record is 1:15. This is pretty good time, actually, and if Betting Tool fails to strut his stuff, she might loom up as the menace of the race.

Pan Flash has bad time for this distance, being four seconds slower than Sometimes Sue, on records from Track X, so we might toss him out of consideration.

Throat Latcher has fair time of 1:17 ⅖ at Track A, a very "fast" track, but he achieved this time carrying only 103 pounds. Today, let's say, he will be carrying 118, a 15-pound package to pick up. This plus his so-so time (on account of the "fastness" of the oval) is enough to eliminate him from the picture.

The case is just about the opposite, however, with Cheap Jack. While this beetle's time at Track A is not much better than that of Throat Latcher, he made that time carrying 120 pounds. Today, he is getting in light ("with a feather"), at, say, only 105 pounds, a 15-pound *drop* in weight. This can make a big difference—and today Cheap Jack might even improve his own best time for the distance considerably.

This kind of checking out of the "best time" factor is absolutely essential if you don't want to be caught flat-footed by a winner you didn't think had a chance in the race. It is always smart to find an animal's *time-weight ratio,* in this manner, as well as his *time-track ratio.* In fact, if you don't do it, you are already on your way to the showers.

Now, there is one more complicating factor—the *time-class ratio*:

It should be clear, by now, that "time is worth only the class it is made in," and that therefore a time of, say, 1:17 is worth a heck of a lot more in a class bracket of $10,000 than it is in a class bracket of $2,000.

So, make one final check of this table, in connection with the past performance charts. Look down the charts and see if, for instance, Sometimes Sue made her time of 1:17 during a period when she was racing at higher class brackets. The charts do not always go back far enough to show these races, but when they do we must be alert to the angle. *For this reason*: If Sometimes Sue made the time of 1:17 with classy horses, she probably made it after being outrun and perhaps eased up. Which means that with cheaper horses (such as those in today's race) she might better this "best time" by two or three seconds! Each animal in the race should be checked out in this way.

All this may sound too "mixed up" to bother with—but actually it's not as complicated as it sounds. It simply means that we must evaluate the "best time" figures by making allowance for weight, track and class difference. Once we do this, we have a pretty good line on who is a possible contender today and who isn't. And this is worth a lot of money for your trouble.

Actually, in practice, you will find that the track differential factor is the most usual cause for surprise. For the general public and the public handicappers—who *should* know better —never take this into account. Here, then, is a terrific angle for any smart handicapper.

If you will carry in your pocket, at all times, the latest "Comparative Track Record Table," clipped from your racing paper, you will put yourself at least 100 giant steps ahead of the general public. For the difference in time for the same distance, between one track and another, can be amazing.

Just to give you an idea, study over this abbreviated table, which is typical of actual track records:

Track		*5½f*	*6f*	*7f*	*1 1/16*	*1 ⅛*
A		1:03⅗	1:08⅘	1:21⅗	1:45⅖	1:47⅕
B		1:05	1:10⅖	1:24⅖	1:46	1:49⅖
C		1:06	1:11⅕	1:26⅖	1:47	1:51
D	*(1)*	*1:02⅖*	*1:08*	*1:20*	*1:39*	*1:46⅘*
E	*(2)*	*1:06¾*	*1:12⅖*	*1:27*	*1:47⅖*	*1:53⅕*

(1) High-class "glamour" track, which has been "skinned" to make it *harder* and *faster*.

(2) Cheap half-mile or "bull-ring" track, with sharp turns.

14. SMART-MONEY HANDICAPPING

THE HANDICAPPING APPROACH set forth in this book differs from the usual methods in a number of important ways, but especially in these:

(1) Handicapping horses on the cold dope ("pure" handicapping) is never good enough to make you a successful player, no matter how well you may be able to spot horses that are in sharp condition, going their best distances, dropping down into soft spots, etc., *because the crucial question of whether or not the trainer is "sending" the horse on a given occasion is left unanswered.* And when this question is left unanswered, everything is left unanswered, and you are unfortunately left in the same position as the player who knows nothing about form reading.

(2) However, to try to pick winners by reading the Tote Board alone, carefully watching the betting action, or lack of it ("handicapping the trainers"), is no good without a knowledge of pure handicapping. Because the betting action is never the last word in the matter, and a trainer can be just as wrong as anybody else about the *winning* chances of his horse. And furthermore, it is often necessary to pick certain horses as losers, despite the fact the stable is betting such animals. They can be picked as losers on the form factors alone. Pure handicapping also is indispensable for spotting "sure-fire" losers, at all times.

Therefore, and this is the whole point of smart handicapping: *smart handicapping is "smart-money" handicapping!* That is to say, it combines a form-reading judgment about the chances of a horse ("pure" handicapping) with the Tote Board action—or lack of it—on this animal. It is a two-way check, a cross-check! Neither the form alone nor the betting action alone is considered to be the last word. *The last word is when a horse checks out on the form AND on the betting action!*

This is how to find the actual contenders in a given horse race.

On the following pages are charts showing horses that move into wins, or near-wins, after losing efforts. *Both the all-out effort and the dull effort could have been spotted in advance, by the principles of "smart-money" handicapping.*

These animals include short-priced winners as well as extreme long-shots, very cheap horses as well as classy ones, races at various distances, different tracks and over different track conditions. The charts are imaginary, but they are typical of the past-performance record of horses running every day of the week on U.S. tracks, and were constructed from a study of thousands of such charts.

You can make you own file of this instructive material by clipping each revealing chart you see from daily racing papers. It is possible to collect a hundred in a matter of weeks.

EXAMPLE NO. 1

Baby Racer (2-year-old filly)

DATE	TRACK	DISTANCE	TIME OF WINNER	TRACK COND.	ODDS	WT.	1ST CALL	2ND CALL	STR.	FINISH	CLASS OF RACE
Jly 7	A	5½ f	1:08	fast	7	116	9-10	7-8	5-4	1-1	5500
Jun 2	A	5 f	1:01⅗	sloppy	38	113	9-8	8-7	6-6	5-2	5500
May 9	B	5 f	1:01⅗	mud	13	115	10-20	9-15	8-15	9-15	Mdn°
Apr 9	C	5 f	1:01	fast	4	118	10-15	10-15	C-13	6-7	6000
Apr 1	C	5 f	:59⅗	good	5	111	8-10	8-13	8-15	8-16	6500

° Maiden race

Comment:

Here is a two-year-old maiden filly that finally moved into a win—July 7—on her fifth try. Note the sharp improvement, *as indicated by the stout late speed,* on June 2, the previous race. This was the first real sign of hot form the animal had shown, in actual racing, since coming out.

However, and this is always worth noting, it appears the stable laid down a heavy bet on her the first time out, April 1, and again on April 9. We know this because of the low odds on those dates, in the absence of any revealed ability. The public will not bet a first-starter, of no particular breeding, down to four or five to one. The stable, of course, knows the animal is burning up the track in morning workouts.

Despite the fact the animal showed sharp form on June 2, we would not have been justified in picking her as a contender on July 7, the winning date, without a strong signal from the Tote Board. *The filly having gone off at 38-1 last start and now going off at 7-1, with no change in class, and only a slight shift in distance—we caught the signal and knew the animal would be there or thereabouts.*

The filly checked out on the form and on the betting action!

On the two previous occasions when the stable bet the horse (April 1 and April 9), we would not have gone along with them. Why? Because we would have been playing in the dark, with no past-performance record to go on. *We must have form signs AND stable intentions.*

In dealing with two-year-olds, so-called "green" racers, the Tote Board must be watched carefully, today, and in previous tries, for signs of stable betting. If the stable misses once or twice, after betting the beetle, they may get a huge mutuel on the day he wins because of the "poor-looking" chart. Two-year-olds tend to improve sharply and suddenly. They explode into a win just about the time you're ready to turn your head and look the other way. If you keep your eye peeled for tiny improvement signs in the charts, however, and weigh the betting action carefully—*you can cash in big on baby racers!*

EXAMPLE NO. 2

Hot Beetle (4-year-old gelding)

DATE	TRACK	DISTANCE	TIME OF WINNER	TRACK COND.	ODDS	WT.	1ST CALL	2ND CALL	STR.	FINISH	CLASS OF RACE
Aug 10	C	6 f	1:11	fast	*3*	117	*5–5*	*4–3*	*3–hd*	*1–2*	*c7000**
Aug 6	C	6 f	1:12⅕	*good*	13	116	*2–1*	*2–1*	4–3	7–5	10000
Jly 23	C	6 f	1:12⅖	*sloppy*	6	120	4–5	6–8	7–12	6–15	10000
Jly 8	C	6 f	1:10⅖	fast	4	116	*1–1*	*1–1*	*1–2*	*1–1*	*c7500*

* c—claimed at price stipulated

Comment:

Here's the type of animal that shows all the signs. He was claimed for $7,500 on July 8, when he proceeded to justify the claimer's good judgment by going out to win handily. The new owner, however, was then a bit too ambitious and sent him back on July 23 for $10,000, a spot that proved a bit too tough. And again, on August 6, when the animal showed good early speed. Both of these races were on "off" tracks which the animal apparently did not like. Also, on these two races the odds rose progressively to 6-1 and then to 13-1, *so it is very likely the stable did not bet.*

However, the stable was waiting for the day. And two tough races at $10,000 served to further condition the horse beautifully for an "all-out" run for the marbles on August 10, at a claiming price of $7,000!

There were no mistakes this day. The stable was shooting for all it was worth, *letting the animal go for a claiming price less than was paid for him.* This was to make sure the spot would be soft enough.

Very often when a stable makes a huge bet on a hot animal, they will drop him in class as a kind of insurance. After all, they may have more money at stake in the mutuel machines than they would lose if somebody decided to claim the horse for $500 or $1,000 less than he cost. *Also, the purse money goes to the man who entered the horse, not to the one claiming him.*

Most horse-players do not pay enough attention to the claim angle in handicapping a race. Remember that when one man claims another man's horse he usually has a good reason for doing so. Being on the inside of the racing business he very often gets it by the grapevine that so-and-so's horse is really showing hot stuff in morning trials. *Also, a claim is usually a pretty good certificate of health for a horse.* Most trainers are not so dumb as to claim a sick or ailing beast.

Whenever you see that a horse is claimed, and then proceeds to show nothing—always ask why. Has he been pitched too high? Run at the wrong distance? Or on footing he does not like? These questions, you will find, pay big dividends!

EXAMPLE NO. 3

In and Outer (4-year-old colt)

DATE	TRACK	DISTANCE	TIME OF WINNER	TRACK COND.	ODDS	WT.	1ST CALL	2ND CALL	STR.	FINISH	CLASS OF RACE
Jun 30	D	6f	1:12⅗	fast	*7*	110	*1–1*	*1–1*	*1–1*	*1–1*	*4500*
Jun 25	D	6f	1:12	fast	26	112	10–9	10–9	10–10	10–15	3500
Jun 12	D	6f	1:11	fast	20	112	1–1	3–2	8–9	12–20	3500
May 26	D	6f	1:12⅗	fast	*5*	110	4–2	*3–1*	*2–1*	*1–1*	*3000*
May 22	D	6f	1:12	fast	19	119	11–10	11–10	10–13	8–8	3000
May 7	D	6f	1:12⅗	fast	12	118	*6–4*	*6–4*	*6–4*	*6–4*	3000
Apr 21	D	6f	1:15⅘	heavy	10	117	2–2	2–1	5–6	7–8	4000
Apr 9	*E*	5f	1:00⅕	fast	*8*	117	*4–2*	*4–2*	*2–1*	*1–2*	*3000*
Mar 17	*E*	5f	1:04	heavy	*15*	122	*4–2*	*3–2*	10–20	9–20	3000

Comment:

When a horse is stepped up in class, even slightly, *the natural tendency is for his odds to rise, not fall!* Therefore, whenever you see the odds fall sharply (below the previous race, or races) on a stepped-up animal, you can rest assured somebody is about to pull a fast one. This is especially true when the animal is showing good speed at the lower claiming brackets, such as the one in this example.

This animal, while showing strong form improvement at $3,500, would not have been a play on June 30, at $4,500, if his odds had risen, say, to 35-1. But the betting action, from the inside, cut the odds down about 75%. This was the double check. *Hot form AND inside bet—despite a step up!* And despite the two previous bad races where there was no try, since the odds rose progressively to 20-1 and 26-1, as they should, on the step-up to $3,500 from $3,000.

The same thing was accomplished by the stable earlier, on May 26, when the animal's odds were cut about 75% from his previous race, just a few days before, on May 22. The hot-form sign came on May 7, when the horse held only four lengths off the pace, all the way around. A similar coup was achieved again back on April 9, at another track, when the animal's odds were cut 50% under the previous race on March 17, when the beetle showed early speed on a heavy track.

Here is a very shrewd stable, indeed. Three tries, three wins. The spots are chosen carefully, and when they feel the animal *can* win, they lay down the dough and let him go! Not many stables can call the shots with such accuracy—but they all try.

It might be well to point out here that *while a step-up or step-down of only $1,000 means very little as far as pure* *handicapping goes, it usually makes a difference on the Tote Board*—which demonstrates the public ignorance about class. The public is composed of one part which believes too much in "class," and another part which believes too little in it!

EXAMPLE NO. 4

Johnny Come Lately (6-year-old horse)

DATE	TRACK	DISTANCE	TIME OF WINNER	TRACK COND.	ODDS	WT.	1ST CALL	2ND CALL	STR.	FINISH	CLASS OF RACE
Jly 15	F	6 f	1:12	fast	29	113	11–13	10–6	5–2	2–hd	2500
Jly 10	F	6 f	1:11	fast	41	113	12–11	11–10	8–10	5–5	2500
Jun 30	F	1 1/16	1:48 1/5	fast	35	114	8–8	9–12	9–15	9–20	2000
Jun 25	F	5 1/2 f	1:06	fast	30	115	10–3	9–7	6–4	4–hd	2500
Jun 16	F	5 1/2 f	1:04	fast	61	115	9–5	8–5	7–11	7–10	2500

Comment:

Here's a beetle that just missed, losing the photo decision by a head when he was going to pay the juicy mutuel, on the win end, of $60.

This animal showed stout late speed on July 10, the previous race, gaining five lengths in the stretch, after a slow beginning. He was 41-1 that day. There was probably no stable bet. But on July 15, the near-hit day, you will note the odds were only 29-1. This indicates inside money, because the chart looks "poor," too poor for either the public or the public handicappers to get aboard. Not one in a hundred of the general public would spot the late-speed sign on July 10. A few "pure" handicappers would see it, but they too would be scared away by the rest of the chart.

It is only by smart-money handicapping that you can catch these eagle-birds!

You will note that the stable loves to do this sort of thing, since the same type of coup was attempted (and failed again) on June 25, at odds of 30-1. *The hot form sign here came on June 16, when the animal was beaten 10 lengths (eased up!) and yet achieved a final time that is still very good!* The final time was 1:06. We get this by adding ⅕ of a second for each beaten length. The time of the race was 1:04.

Likewise, a final-time analysis of the race on July 10 shows the animal capable of running six furlongs in 1:12 flat. He was beaten only five lengths in a time of 1:11 flat. So, he figured right in there on July 15, just as he did on June 25, at the shorter distance.

It is necessary to use your judgment carefully on the matter of spotting a stable bet or the lack of it. *Just because a horse is at high odds, do not assume the stable is not betting.* Ask this question: Is the price high in relation to what it ought to be, considering the appearance of the chart? Actually, it might be low in relation to what it would be if there were no stable bet. Remember that when a horse runs back a few times, no public handicapper will pick him, even though a careful analysis of the race might show he was making a good effort. Therefore, if his odds drop despite this lack of favoritism—*then the money has to be coming from the inside!*

EXAMPLE NO. 5

Lawn Mower (5-year-old horse)

DATE	TRACK	DISTANCE	TIME OF WINNER	TRACK COND.	ODDS	WT.	1ST CALL	2ND CALL	STR.	FINISH	CLASS OF RACE
Jly 10	*A*	*tc1 1/16*	1:47 3/5	firm	*7*	117	*3–1*	*1–4*	*1–4*	*1–1*	*5500*
Jun 27	Y	1 1/16	1:47 4/5	fast	12	117	5–4	12–10	12–15	12–20	3500
Jun 22	*Y*	*tc1 1/16**	1:46 2/5	firm	*15*	119	*2–1*	*4–2*	*7–12*	*9–15*	*5000*
Jun 20	A	6 f	1:12 2/5	fast	3	116	9–7	9–7	10–8	10–9	3500
Jun 8	A	1	1:39 2/5	fast	4	119	1–hd	7–7	7–9	7–10	4500

* tc—Turf Course

Comment:

Even *a slight drop* in the odds (from the previous race) when a horse is stepped-up should give us pause. The natural tendency is always for the odds to *rise* on a stepped-up animal. Why do they fall? Neither the public nor the public handicappers will go for such an animal. They avoid him like the plague, especially when he has been running far back at lower brackets. So, most definitely, the money comes from the insiders, the stable or the stable-connection professionals. *This is the strongest kind of tip you will ever get on a horse race—and the most reliable!*

In this example, the stable (a shrewd one) *worked a switcheroo from the turf to the dirt track and back to the turf,* knowing all along the horse was favored by the turf course. The nice price of 7-1, on the July 10 win, was "built" by the stable, just as you would build a booby-trap, beginning on June 22.

On this date, two races back, at another track, the animal was run on the turf where he showed a bit of early foot in what was probably nothing more than a "workout" for him, to get the feel of the grass. There was no stable bet, since the animal's odds rose (over previous races) as they figured to do, on the step-up alone. *The only conclusion is that on June 22, the animal was not being "sent."* He was being prepped for the big day. On June 27, he was run at the distance on the dirt track, and the odds dropped (as they should with a drop in class) but there was no stable bet. *This lousy race was to tell the public handicappers and the public that the horse was "out of form."*

So, comes the big day—July 10—and the animal is stepped-up good (by $2,000). The race is on the turf, and the marbles are laid down!

How do we know all this to be true? Well, it's a fairly logical deduction from the cold facts in the case. Despite the animal's bad performance on the turf less than three weeks previously, and the miserable race in-between, his odds are cut to less than half what they were on June 22. In the absense of a huge stable bet on the July 10 effort, this beetle's odds would have been at least 25 or 30-1!

EXAMPLE NO. 6

Cheap Jack (3-year-old colt)

DATE	TRACK	DISTANCE	TIME OF WINNER	TRACK COND.	ODDS	WT.	1ST CALL	2ND CALL	STR.	FINISH	CLASS OF RACE
Jly 10	*F*	6 f	1:12⅕	fast	*6*	*112*	*1–1*	*1–2*	*1–3*	*1–5*	*2500*
Jly 6	*F*	6 f	1:12⅖	fast	2*	113	2–1	4–1	7–3	7–9	*2500*
Jun 24	G	6 f	*1:10⅗*	fast	*12*	114	3–2	3–3	5–9	7–11	*4500*
Jun 15	G	6 f	1:11	fast	*16*	111	2–2	4–2	4–5	8–7	4500
May 20	G	6 f	1:13⅕	good	*19*	112	2–*1*	2–*1*	5–4	12–10	4500

* Tote Board favorite in the race.

Comment:

Here's a typical maneuver used by many stables to get a good mutuel price on a horse *when they decide to step-down and win.* The animal was coming into form at a claiming price of $4,500. On May 20 he showed a bit of early speed. On June 15, he showed even more. On June 24, *he showed good early speed on a very fast pace* (note the hot time of the race: 1:10 ⅗). In all these races there was probably no stable bet because the colt was not considered ready. The odds were 19-1, 16-1 and 12-1 respectively. Just the slight kind of drop in odds you would expect from public betting alone.

On July 6, the animal was started at another track and dropped down to $2,500. Obviously, with an improving animal, this was a soft spot if the stable wanted to win. The previous race (June 24) showed a final time of 1:12⅘, even though the beetle was beaten by 11 lengths. The final time of 1:12⅘ in a class bracket of $4,500 made the animal a top contender on July 6, at the cheaper bracket of $2,500—and the public handicappers were quick to make him the favorite. *Therefore, there was heavy betting this day by the public.*

Did the stable bet? Our guess would be they didn't bet a dime. Because it is very unlikely they would "send" an animal under these circumstances. All trainers know that when you blow *on* a drop-down you get a good price the next try. So why, with the public jumping all over your horse—why would you win at 2-1 or 3-1, when you can get 6-1 (*sometimes far more*) by waiting a few days.

Also, note that the animal blows on the first start at a new track. This protects the stable from the wrath of the stewards for such shenanigans. Remember there is an unwritten law that excuses the bad performance of a horse first time out at a new track. Trainers are always taking advantage of this.

The general rule of thumb that the odds should fall on a stepped-down animal must be qualified—naturally—when an animal has been manipulated to produce a rise in the odds. You must always ask yourself whether an animal has been "dogged" or "stiffed" to produce just this result.

EXAMPLE NO. 7

Roy the Router (9-year-old gelding)

DATE	TRACK	DISTANCE	TIME OF WINNER	TRACK COND.	ODDS	WT.	1ST CALL	2ND CALL	STR.	FINISH	CLASS OF RACE
Aug 14	I	1¹⁄₁₆	1:48⅘	fast	12	117	3–4	3–3	3–1	1–2	2500
Aug 10	I	6½ f	1:20	fast	41	115	7–7	7–6	4–3	10–12	3500
Aug 1	I	1⅛	1:56⅘	fast	16	117	1–1	2–1	3–1	7–11	2000
Jly 30	I	1¹⁄₁₆	1:51	slow	9	117	9–6	2–hd	7–4	10–12	2000

Comment:

The *wrong* distance can make a horse lose, and the *right* distance can help him to win—when he's in condition. Very often an animal is brought into winning form by racing him at a distance too long or too short for his best performance. Then, when he is ready to win, he is entered at the proper distance and the stable bets a bundle, as can be seen in this example.

The animal began showing signs of form on July 30, when he moved up with a rush to be only a head off the leader, at the mile pole, and then flattened out. The animal was "short" and needed an endurance build-up. So, on August 1 he was run at one mile and one eighth, a distance somewhat too long for his best performance. In this race he ran well all the way into the stretch, where he was eased up. It was now clear to the stable that the beast was ready to win at one mile and one-sixteenth.

So, instead of getting impatient and greedy for a win, the stable played it cool. *They knew that if they came right back, at a somewhat shorter distance, the public handicappers would be sure to spot the animal as a contender and point him out to the public in black-face type.* Therefore, to confuse the issue and make the animal look bad, they ran him back on August 10 at six-and-one-half furlongs (6½ f), a distance clearly too short. Just to make sure he would look bad on this day, they stepped him up, at the same time, to $3,500.

All this had the desired effect. The animal, going the wrong distance and entered over his head, was severely beaten. Yet, if you look closely, you will note that even so, he moved up to fourth in the stretch before he was clobbered out of contention.

So, on August 14, with the public thrown off the trail,

the animal was dropped slightly (for insurance), entered at his very proper distance and sent out for the sugar. He got there at the very nice mutuel of $26, and the stable no doubt won enough to pay his feed bill *for the next year!*

In other words, the stable got 12-1 on the win, by waiting and fooling the public with an in-between lousy race, instead of the 2-1 or 3-1 they would have got by winning as soon as they could have. These are the rewards of patience!

EXAMPLE NO. 8

Mud in Your Eye (4-year-old colt)

DATE	TRACK	DISTANCE	TIME OF WINNER	TRACK COND.	ODDS	WT.	1ST CALL	2ND CALL	STR.	FINISH	CLASS OF RACE
Jly 11	C	1	1:38$\frac{3}{5}$	*muddy*	*8*	114	*6–2*	*3–1*	*2–hd*	*1–2*	*4000*
Jly 2	C	1	1:36$\frac{2}{5}$	fast	41	114	6–5	6–6	6–6	6–8	5500
Jun 27	C	7 f	1:22$\frac{3}{5}$	fast	40	116	10–12	9–9	8–8	8–15	5000
Jun 20	C	7 f	1:25	*muddy*	26	111	*1–1*	*1–1*	5–8	10–15	*c4000**
Jun 8	C	1	1:35$\frac{3}{5}$	fast	8	114	4–2	4–3	5–5	6–5	5000

* c—claimed at price stipulated

Comment:

Mud will make a difference in the way some horses run—if they are ready to run anyway. If they are out of form, or not yet in their best form to win, mud will not help them too much. The way to spot a horse that will run in the mud today is not by mud marks (the familiar "X" after his name in racing papers) but by spotting the inside bet on the beast.

In this example we see a smart win in the mud, with the stable betting strongly. On July 11, the winning date, the odds go to 8-1, as against 41-1 and 40-1 on the two previous races, in which there was no try. *These two previous races at higher class brackets were strictly conditioning races, to bring the animal to peak for the eventual drop-down and win.*

The race—in the mud—on June 20 was the form tip-off. The animal led the race for a half mile. He wasn't ready to win yet, but he was on the upgrade. There was no stable bet. A second stable, smelling a good thing, claimed the beetle.

Most animals which are claimed tend to show something before too long, thus revealing the reason they were bought up in the first place. When one trainer claims another man's horse, it is because he knows the animal is improving rapidly. He knows this, from astute form reading, or from morning workouts he has seen or heard about, or from other more complex indications.

As for mud-running ability—some animals have it and others do not. *However, to confuse the issue, some animals will run in the mud when they are feeling good, but refuse it when they are feeling bad.* So, to let yourself be guided by "mud marks" is a sure way to go broke. Many animals who do not have "mud marks" love the mud.

When the track is "off"—sloppy, slow or muddy to heavy—

let yourself be guided by signs of form improvement and by signs of stable money, not by anything so vague as a "mud-mark."

Most trainers can be trusted to know whether a horse will refuse a certain type of wet track. So, when they lay down their marbles on a horse, on an "off" track, you can safely go along, if the other signs are present.

EXAMPLE NO. 9

Steady Steve (6-year-old gelding)

DATE	TRACK	DISTANCE	TIME OF WINNER	TRACK COND.	ODDS	WT.	1ST CALL	2ND CALL	STR.	FINISH	CLASS OF RACE
Jly 10	Y	1¹⁄₁₆	1:44⅖	fast	5	115	1-1	1-2	1-2	1-1	10000
Jun 22	Y	1¹⁄₁₆	1:46	fast	10	116	1-1	2-hd	3-1	4-1	7500
May 26	Z	1¹⁄₁₆	1:46⅖	fast	8	117	1-hd	2-1	3-1	5-1	7500
May 13	Z	1¹⁄₁₆	1:46	fast	16	116	4-3	3-3	3-3	3-3	7500
May 5	Z	1¹⁄₁₆	1:45	fast	20	114	5-5	5-8	5-6	5-7	9500

Comment:

Here is an example of a horse which has excellent time for the distance, but this fact is overlooked by the public *because of a change of tracks*. The stable knew all about it however, and socked in the dough, despite a step-up, on the winning trip.

This animal improved his time on July 10 almost two full seconds over his good race of June 22. But this was no surprise to the stable. He figured to improve—because he has high speed for one mile and one sixteenth ($1\frac{1}{16}$). A glance down the chart will show three stout races at Track Z, where the track record for this distance is 1:44 as against 1:42 for Track Y. Track Y therefore is a much "faster" track than Track Z—so the animal was bound to run "faster" at Track Y, sooner or later.

The trick here is the variation of time from one track to another, while running at the same speed.

It is safe to say that not one horse-player in a hundred ever takes this fact about track surface, or track contour, into consideration. And yet, all you have to do is to clip from your racing paper the table which shows the track records for various distances at each of the major tracks. By keeping this handy for reference, you can always check out the true speed of animals which are being shifted from one track to another.

The example given here works in reverse, naturally. *If an animal with fast time at Track Y moves over to Track Z you can expect his time to get "slower."*

A word of caution here is necessary, however. Sometimes a trainer does not try on the first time out at a new track, since by blowing the first one he can get a nice mutuel on the second, or even third try. In the example here it appears there was no try on the first attempt at Track Y, June 22, since the odds rose to 10-1. This is high, considering the pretty good parting effort at Track Z, where he was 8-1.

On the winning trip, July 10, the animal was stepped up to $10,000 and his odds went to 5-1, just exactly half what they were last time—in a class bracket of $7,500. *There is no question of a stable bet when you see something like this!*

Once again, we repeat, the odds on a stepped up animal should *rise—not fall!*

EXAMPLE NO. 10

Betting Tool (5-year-old gelding)

DATE	TRACK	DISTANCE	TIME OF WINNER	TRACK COND.	ODDS	WT.	1ST CALL	2ND CALL	STR.	FINISH	CLASS OF RACE
Jly 16	F	6 f	1:11⅖	fast	48	112	1–1	1–2	1–3	1–5	3500
Jly 1	F	6 f	1:13	fast	4	120	5–6	6–7	8–9	12–20	2000
Jun 25	F	6 f	1:12	fast	5	115	9–10	9–15	9–20	9–20	2500
Jun 12	F	6 f	1:11⅘	fast	20	110	1–1	1–1	1–1	1–2	3000
Jun 6	M	6½ f	1:19⅖	fast	5	106	7–8	8–9	9–9	10–10	2000
Jun 1	M	6½ f	1:19	fast	18	112	1–1	1–1	1–2	1–hd	2000

Comment:

Here's a beetle that paid a cute mutuel of almost $100. Did the stable bet him—or was it a big surprise to everybody?

We would say it was a big surprise to almost everybody *except* the stable. *There is plenty of evidence to suggest the stable is one that specializes in winning at big odds.* On June 12, they hit at 20-1. And on June 1, at 18-1. When you see an animal with this pattern, you know you are dealing with a shrewd gambling outfit. The big mystery about a stable like this one is how they avoid being kicked out of the business by the track stewards. *The "stiffing" of the animal, when the price is short, is too obvious!*

How is it possible, you might say, for a horse to pay $100 if the stable bet him. Surely they couldn't have bet much!

At a major track, where there is a huge betting pool, it is very possible for a horse with a poor-looking chart (on his immediately previous races) to pay $100, or more, with the stable making a bet, even a sizeable bet. The abnormally high mutuel comes from emotional betting by the public on other horses in the race. Sometimes the public handicappers will make a certain horse (or perhaps two) such an outstanding choice that the price on everything else gets out of line. This produces a few extreme overlays on the Tote Board.

The animal, and the stable, in this example, was the beneficiary of such foolish sheep-like betting by the public. His odds should have been no more than about 15-1, because he had shown talent for a class bracket of $3,000 (on June 12) and had won smartly!

Well, you might say, logically enough, "If his odds should have been no more than 15-1, how could we possibly spot such a beast as a contender?"

There is only one answer to this good question: *when you recognize that you are dealing with a stable like this, you must be willing to go against the usual rules of thumb.* Just as you must, also, in a case where you believe an animal is going to be "stiffed." *If the odds go abnormally low on an animal, you always run the risk the stable may not "send" the beast.*

In these matters, there is no substitute for using your head and making good judgments!

MELVIN POWERS SELF-IMPROVEMENT LIBRARY

ASTROLOGY

___ ASTROLOGY: HOW TO CHART YOUR HOROSCOPE *Max Heindel*	5.00
___ ASTROLOGY AND SEXUAL ANALYSIS *Morris C. Goodman*	5.00
___ ASTROLOGY AND YOU *Carroll Righter*	5.00
___ ASTROLOGY MADE EASY *Astarte*	5.00
___ ASTROLOGY, ROMANCE, YOU AND THE STARS *Anthony Norvell*	5.00
___ MY WORLD OF ASTROLOGY *Sydney Omarr*	7.00
___ THOUGHT DIAL *Sydney Omarr*	7.00
___ WHAT THE STARS REVEAL ABOUT THE MEN IN YOUR LIFE *Thelma White*	3.00

BRIDGE

___ BRIDGE BIDDING MADE EASY *Edwin B. Kantar*	10.00
___ BRIDGE CONVENTIONS *Edwin B. Kantar*	7.00
___ COMPETITIVE BIDDING IN MODERN BRIDGE *Edgar Kaplan*	7.00
___ DEFENSIVE BRIDGE PLAY COMPLETE *Edwin B. Kantar*	15.00
___ GAMESMAN BRIDGE—PLAY BETTER WITH KANTAR *Edwin B. Kantar*	5.00
___ HOW TO IMPROVE YOUR BRIDGE *Alfred Sheinwold*	5.00
___ IMPROVING YOUR BIDDING SKILLS *Edwin B. Kantar*	4.00
___ INTRODUCTION TO DECLARER'S PLAY *Edwin B. Kantar*	7.00
___ INTRODUCTION TO DEFENDER'S PLAY *Edwin B. Kantar*	7.00
___ KANTAR FOR THE DEFENSE *Edwin B. Kantar*	7.00
___ KANTAR FOR THE DEFENSE VOLUME 2 *Edwin B. Kantar*	7.00
___ TEST YOUR BRIDGE PLAY *Edwin B. Kantar*	5.00
___ VOLUME 2—TEST YOUR BRIDGE PLAY *Edwin B. Kantar*	7.00
___ WINNING DECLARER PLAY *Dorothy Hayden Truscott*	7.00

BUSINESS, STUDY & REFERENCE

___ BRAINSTORMING *Charles Clark*	7.00
___ CONVERSATION MADE EASY *Elliot Russell*	4.00
___ EXAM SECRET *Dennis B. Jackson*	3.00
___ FIX-IT BOOK *Arthur Symons*	2.00
___ HOW TO DEVELOP A BETTER SPEAKING VOICE *M. Hellier*	4.00
___ HOW TO SELF-PUBLISH YOUR BOOK & MAKE IT A BEST SELLER *Melvin Powers*	10.00
___ INCREASE YOUR LEARNING POWER *Geoffrey A. Dudley*	3.00
___ PRACTICAL GUIDE TO BETTER CONCENTRATION *Melvin Powers*	3.00
___ PRACTICAL GUIDE TO PUBLIC SPEAKING *Maurice Forley*	5.00
___ 7 DAYS TO FASTER READING *William S. Schaill*	5.00
___ SONGWRITERS' RHYMING DICTIONARY *Jane Shaw Whitfield*	7.00
___ SPELLING MADE EASY *Lester D. Basch & Dr. Milton Finkelstein*	3.00
___ STUDENT'S GUIDE TO BETTER GRADES *J. A. Rickard*	3.00
___ TEST YOURSELF—FIND YOUR HIDDEN TALENT *Jack Shafer*	3.00
___ YOUR WILL & WHAT TO DO ABOUT IT *Attorney Samuel G. Kling*	5.00

CALLIGRAPHY

___ ADVANCED CALLIGRAPHY *Katherine Jeffares*	7.00
___ CALLIGRAPHER'S REFERENCE BOOK *Anne Leptich & Jacque Evans*	7.00
___ CALLIGRAPHY—THE ART OF BEAUTIFUL WRITING *Katherine Jeffares*	7.00
___ CALLIGRAPHY FOR FUN & PROFIT *Anne Leptich & Jacque Evans*	7.00
___ CALLIGRAPHY MADE EASY *Tina Serafini*	7.00

CHESS & CHECKERS

___ BEGINNER'S GUIDE TO WINNING CHESS *Fred Reinfeld*	5.00
___ CHESS IN TEN EASY LESSONS *Larry Evans*	5.00
___ CHESS MADE EASY *Milton L. Hanauer*	5.00
___ CHESS PROBLEMS FOR BEGINNERS *Edited by Fred Reinfeld*	5.00
___ CHESS TACTICS FOR BEGINNERS *Edited by Fred Reinfeld*	5.00
___ CHESS THEORY & PRACTICE *Morry & Mitchell*	2.00
___ HOW TO WIN AT CHECKERS *Fred Reinfeld*	5.00

___ HOW TO PICK WINNING HORSES *Bob McKnight*		5.00
___ HOW TO WIN AT THE RACES *Sam (The Genius) Lewin*		5.00
___ HOW YOU CAN BEAT THE RACES *Jack Kavanagh*		5.00
___ MAKING MONEY AT THE RACES *David Barr*		5.00
___ PAYDAY AT THE RACES *Les Conklin*		5.00
___ SMART HANDICAPPING MADE EASY *William Bauman*		5.00
___ SUCCESS AT THE HARNESS RACES *Barry Meadow*		5.00
___ WINNING AT THE HARNESS RACES—AN EXPERT'S GUIDE *Nick Cammarano*		5.00

HUMOR

___ HOW TO FLATTEN YOUR TUSH *Coach Marge Reardon*		2.00
___ HOW TO MAKE LOVE TO YOURSELF *Ron Stevens & Joy Grdnic*		3.00
___ JOKE TELLER'S HANDBOOK *Bob Orben*		7.00
___ JOKES FOR ALL OCCASIONS *Al Schock*		5.00
___ 2,000 NEW LAUGHS FOR SPEAKERS *Bob Orben*		5.00
___ 2,500 JOKES TO START 'EM LAUGHING *Bob Orben*		5.00

HYPNOTISM

___ ADVANCED TECHNIQUES OF HYPNOSIS *Melvin Powers*		3.00
___ CHILDBIRTH WITH HYPNOSIS *William S. Kroger, M.D.*		5.00
___ HOW TO SOLVE YOUR SEX PROBLEMS WITH SELF-HYPNOSIS *Frank S. Caprio, M.D.*		5.00
___ HOW TO STOP SMOKING THRU SELF-HYPNOSIS *Leslie M. LeCron*		3.00
___ HOW TO USE AUTO-SUGGESTION EFFECTIVELY *John Duckworth*		3.00
___ HOW YOU CAN BOWL BETTER USING SELF-HYPNOSIS *Jack Heise*		4.00
___ HOW YOU CAN PLAY BETTER GOLF USING SELF-HYPNOSIS *Jack Heise*		3.00
___ HYPNOSIS AND SELF-HYPNOSIS *Bernard Hollander, M.D.*		5.00
___ HYPNOTISM *(Originally published in 1893) Carl Sextus*		5.00
___ HYPNOTISM & PSYCHIC PHENOMENA *Simeon Edmunds*		4.00
___ HYPNOTISM MADE EASY *Dr. Ralph Winn*		5.00
___ HYPNOTISM MADE PRACTICAL *Louis Orton*		5.00
___ HYPNOTISM REVEALED *Melvin Powers*		3.00
___ HYPNOTISM TODAY *Leslie LeCron and Jean Bordeaux, Ph.D.*		5.00
___ MODERN HYPNOSIS *Lesley Kuhn & Salvatore Russo, Ph.D.*		5.00
___ NEW CONCEPTS OF HYPNOSIS *Bernard C. Gindes, M.D.*		7.00
___ NEW SELF-HYPNOSIS *Paul Adams*		7.00
___ POST-HYPNOTIC INSTRUCTIONS—SUGGESTIONS FOR THERAPY *Arnold Furst*		5.00
___ PRACTICAL GUIDE TO SELF-HYPNOSIS *Melvin Powers*		3.00
___ PRACTICAL HYPNOTISM *Philip Magonet, M.D.*		3.00
___ SECRETS OF HYPNOTISM *S. J. Van Pelt, M.D.*		5.00
___ SELF-HYPNOSIS—A CONDITIONED-RESPONSE TECHNIQUE *Laurence Sparks*		7.00
___ SELF-HYPNOSIS—ITS THEORY, TECHNIQUE & APPLICATION *Melvin Powers*		3.00
___ THERAPY THROUGH HYPNOSIS *Edited by Raphael H. Rhodes*		5.00

JUDAICA

___ SERVICE OF THE HEART *Evelyn Garfiel, Ph.D.*		7.00
___ STORY OF ISRAEL IN COINS *Jean & Maurice Gould*		2.00
___ STORY OF ISRAEL IN STAMPS *Maxim & Gabriel Shamir*		1.00
___ TONGUE OF THE PROPHETS *Robert St. John*		7.00

JUST FOR WOMEN

___ COSMOPOLITAN'S GUIDE TO MARVELOUS MEN Foreword by *Helen Gurley Brown*		3.00
___ COSMOPOLITAN'S HANG-UP HANDBOOK Foreword by *Helen Gurley Brown*		4.00
___ COSMOPOLITAN'S LOVE BOOK—A GUIDE TO ECSTASY IN BED		7.00
___ COSMOPOLITAN'S NEW ETIQUETTE GUIDE Foreword by *Helen Gurley Brown*		4.00
___ I AM A COMPLEAT WOMAN *Doris Hagopian & Karen O'Connor Sweeney*		3.00
___ JUST FOR WOMEN—A GUIDE TO THE FEMALE BODY *Richard E. Sand, M.D.*		5.00
___ NEW APPROACHES TO SEX IN MARRIAGE *John E. Eichenlaub, M.D.*		3.00
___ SEXUALLY ADEQUATE FEMALE *Frank S. Caprio, M.D.*		3.00
___ SEXUALLY FULFILLED WOMAN *Dr. Rachel Copelan*		5.00
___ YOUR FIRST YEAR OF MARRIAGE *Dr. Tom McGinnis*		3.00

__ KNIGHT IN THE RUSTY ARMOR *Robert Fisher*		5.00
__ LEFT-HANDED PEOPLE *Michael Barsley*		5.00
__ MAGIC IN YOUR MIND *U.S. Andersen*		7.00
__ MAGIC OF THINKING BIG *Dr. David J. Schwartz*		3.00
__ MAGIC OF THINKING SUCCESS *Dr. David J. Schwartz*		7.00
__ MAGIC POWER OF YOUR MIND *Walter M. Germain*		7.00
__ MENTAL POWER THROUGH SLEEP SUGGESTION *Melvin Powers*		3.00
__ NEVER UNDERESTIMATE THE SELLING POWER OF A WOMAN *Dottie Walters*		7.00
__ NEW GUIDE TO RATIONAL LIVING *Albert Ellis, Ph.D. & R. Harper, Ph.D.*		7.00
__ PSYCHO-CYBERNETICS *Maxwell Maltz, M.D.*		7.00
__ PSYCHOLOGY OF HANDWRITING *Nadya Olyanova*		7.00
__ SALES CYBERNETICS *Brian Adams*		7.00
__ SCIENCE OF MIND IN DAILY LIVING *Dr. Donald Curtis*		7.00
__ SECRET OF SECRETS *U.S. Andersen*		7.00
__ SECRET POWER OF THE PYRAMIDS *U. S. Andersen*		7.00
__ SELF-THERAPY FOR THE STUTTERER *Malcolm Frazer*		3.00
__ SUCCESS-CYBERNETICS *U. S. Andersen*		7.00
__ 10 DAYS TO A GREAT NEW LIFE *William E. Edwards*		3.00
__ THINK AND GROW RICH *Napoleon Hill*		7.00
__ THINK YOUR WAY TO SUCCESS *Dr. Lew Losoncy*		5.00
__ THREE MAGIC WORDS *U. S. Andersen*		7.00
__ TREASURY OF COMFORT *Edited by Rabbi Sidney Greenberg*		7.00
__ TREASURY OF THE ART OF LIVING *Sidney S. Greenberg*		7.00
__ WHAT YOUR HANDWRITING REVEALS *Albert E. Hughes*		3.00
__ YOUR SUBCONSCIOUS POWER *Charles M. Simmons*		7.00
__ YOUR THOUGHTS CAN CHANGE YOUR LIFE *Dr. Donald Curtis*		7.00

SPORTS

__ BICYCLING FOR FUN AND GOOD HEALTH *Kenneth E. Luther*		2.00
__ BILLIARDS—POCKET • CAROM • THREE CUSION *Clive Cottingham, Jr.*		5.00
__ COMPLETE GUIDE TO FISHING *Vlad Evanoff*		2.00
__ HOW TO IMPROVE YOUR RACQUETBALL *Lubarsky, Kaufman & Scagnetti*		5.00
__ HOW TO WIN AT POCKET BILLIARDS *Edward D. Knuchell*		7.00
__ JOY OF WALKING *Jack Scagnetti*		3.00
__ LEARNING & TEACHING SOCCER SKILLS *Eric Worthington*		3.00
__ MOTORCYCLING FOR BEGINNERS *I.G. Edmonds*		3.00
__ RACQUETBALL FOR WOMEN *Toni Hudson, Jack Scagnetti & Vince Rondone*		3.00
__ RACQUETBALL MADE EASY *Steve Lubarsky, Rod Delson & Jack Scagnetti*		5.00
__ SECRET OF BOWLING STRIKES *Dawson Taylor*		5.00
__ SECRET OF PERFECT PUTTING *Horton Smith & Dawson Taylor*		5.00
__ SOCCER—THE GAME & HOW TO PLAY IT *Gary Rosenthal*		5.00
__ STARTING SOCCER *Edward F. Dolan, Jr.*		5.00

TENNIS LOVER'S LIBRARY

__ BEGINNER'S GUIDE TO WINNING TENNIS *Helen Hull Jacobs*		2.00
__ HOW TO BEAT BETTER TENNIS PLAYERS *Loring Fiske*		4.00
__ HOW TO IMPROVE YOUR TENNIS—STYLE, STRATEGY & ANALYSIS *C. Wilson*		2.00
__ PSYCH YOURSELF TO BETTER TENNIS *Dr. Walter A. Luszki*		2.00
__ TENNIS FOR BEGINNERS *Dr. H. A. Murray*		2.00
__ TENNIS MADE EASY *Joel Brecheen*		5.00
__ WEEKEND TENNIS—HOW TO HAVE FUN & WIN AT THE SAME TIME *Bill Talbert*		3.00
__ WINNING WITH PERCENTAGE TENNIS—SMART STRATEGY *Jack Lowe*		2.00

WILSHIRE PET LIBRARY

__ DOG OBEDIENCE TRAINING *Gust Kessopulos*		5.00
__ DOG TRAINING MADE EASY & FUN *John W. Kellogg*		5.00
__ HOW TO BRING UP YOUR PET DOG *Kurt Unkelbach*		2.00
__ HOW TO RAISE & TRAIN YOUR PUPPY *Jeff Griffen*		5.00

he books listed above can be obtained from your book dealer or directly from Melvin Powers.
hen ordering, please remit $1.50 postage for the first book and 50¢ for each additional book.

Melvin Powers
12015 Sherman Road, No. Hollywood, California 91605